I AM A SOME BODY

Emerging From

the Shadows

SHARON SCHMITZ

Published by BookBaby

7905 N Crescent Blvd.

Pennsauken, NJ 08110

Library of Congress Cataloging-in-Publication Data

Author: Schmitz, Sharon, 1932-author; sschmitz@sistersofmercy.org

Title: I am a Somebody: Emerging From the Shadows

Printed in the United States of America

By BabyBook

7905 N Crescent Blvd.

Pennsauken, NJ 08110

©2022 Sharon Schmitz

ISBN: 978-1-66782-976-0

ACKNOWLEDGEMENTS

*T*his book could never have been written were it not for generous funding by the Sisters of Mercy of the Americas. I am especially grateful to Sisters Jane Mary Hotstream, Mary Rose Bumpus, Debbie Kern, and Pat Coward, leaders of what was, at that time, the South Central Community of the Sisters of Mercy. Their encouragement and support for this project made this funding available.

I am grateful, also, to the women who edited the manuscript at various stages of its development. They were Professor Barbara Baumgartner, Washington University in St. Louis who organized the manuscript's content in its early beginnings, Karel Lucander who edited the Introduction, and Mercy Sisters Paulinus Oakes and Sarah Ducey who edited the manuscript at various stages of its development. In addition, Sarah's computer expertise lifted me out of many computer jams.

I thank the many friends who read parts of the manuscript, listened to my sharing of some of the stories, and insisted that these stories must be shared.

I suffered a CVA (stroke) while writing this book. I owe great thanks to Sister Michaelanne Estoup who recognized that I was experiencing a health crisis. She and Sister Lalemant Pelikan, rushed me to Mercy Hospital, St. Louis, so quickly that the emergency room physician and his staff were able to preserve my mental faculties. That physician has, since that time, moved to another state. I regret that I do not know his whereabouts to thank him and send him a copy of this book.

A special "hats off" to Tanya Bishop, Activities Director at Catherine's Residence, and "jill of all trades." She responded, without hesitation and with tender mercy to my request for computer assistance. Her expertise organized and bundled together the various elements of this manuscript and readied it for publication. Were it not for Tanya, this book would not be in your hands today.

I do not have sufficient words to express my gratitude to Sister Richard Mary Burke, RSM and Ms Ruth Dotson whose unwavering support opened all necessary doors to make possible the publication of this book. They are a great blessing to me.

The stories in this book were offered to me by the justice-involved-women who enrolled in my course, *Becoming All We Can Be,* in the Buzz Westfall Justice Center in Clayton MO. My gratitude, love and appreciation of them is unending. I pray that their life stories will convince readers and legislators that women's penal institutions must be transformed into healing centers.

TABLE OF CONTENTS

INTRODUCTION:

I AM A SOMEBODY:
EMERGING FROM THE SHADOWS

*S*tatistics are like flashlights. They illuminate one corner of a situation while shadowing the rest. They state the observables – the WHO's and WHAT's of situations - but the WHY's beneath the surface remain hidden.

For example, 2018 statistics state bald facts:

- 231,000 females in U.S. jails and prisons.
- over 1,000,000 females on probation and parole.
- over 2,000,000 of their children in "kincare".

This data creates negative judgments in our mind, and a foul taste in our mouth. No wonder folks say, "Lock them up and throw away the key!"

That's how I felt before I heard these women's stories. The statistics closed my mind, but the stories melted my heart.

The deceased East Indian Jesuit priest, Anthony DeMello wrote: "The shortest distance between a human being and the truth is a story."

This is a book of stories - stories to open our hearts and minds to what statistics cannot reveal – experiences that traumatized the youthful years of justice-involved-women. When adults doled out harm, instead of love, to the girl children in their care, the youth sought refuge in unhealthy relationships which led them into prostitution, drugs and crime.

During the years I taught these women, my mind ached to let the public see them as they really are: victims more than offenders. To that end, I invited the women to write their early life stories for me. I wanted readers to see the traumas that incubated their crimes.

The women gave me permission to include their stories in this book with the understanding that I would change their names. I have also changed the names of the friends and family members who peopled their lives.

I offer these stories and the accompanying data to you with the hope that they will:

- clothe the statistics in flesh and bone,
- illustrate that incarcerating, without healing underlying traumas, is short-sighted, ineffective, and unjust,
- shock you with the types and extent of violence – and, yes, crimes – committed against women during incarceration, and
- advocate for restorative/transformative (healing) processes to replace retributive (harmful) processes in U.S. society.

This book can hold only a limited number of stories, so be aware that the stories herein represent the traumatic early lives of thousands and tens of thousands of other jailed women.

Writers have a two-fold responsibility: to be true to facts while also presenting a book's contents in a readable, enjoyable format. To facilitate easy reading, I deleted repetitious and irrelevant content in the stories and re-arranged some data to better clarify facts. I chose not to correct spelling or reconstruct sentences when the errors better illustrated a woman's challenges.

Verification of stories is a difficult task. In most instances, after a woman submitted her story, I interviewed her to clarify the information. When it seemed helpful, I integrated information from interviews and homework into the written stories. Insofar as possible, I consulted other sources (family members, newspaper accounts, information on the websites of the Department of Corrections and Case.Net) to verify some of the written accounts. I also sought consistency between the written stories, verbal statements made in the classroom, and data found in the women's class-work. Understandably, private childhood and teen traumas cannot be fact-checked for accuracy.

It is important to note that I had the privilege of spending 13 hours in class with each woman plus approximately five additional hours reviewing her homework and interviewing her.

These stories came from women jailed in the Buzz Westfall Justice Center in St. Louis. Most, but not all, of the women are residents of Missouri. (Those having residence in other states are in the Buzz Westfall Justice Center because their crimes occurred in St. Louis County.)

Approximately half are stories of U.S. white women, 1/4th U.S. women of color, and the remaining 1/4th, women of mixed-race parentage.

None of the women was offered payment or gifts for her story. I did offer to give each of them a copy of this book if I knew her whereabouts at the time of the book's publication.

I am the major co-founder of St. Louis's Center for Women in Transition (CWIT), an organization which provides comprehensive wraparound services including supportive housing; case management; life skills education; behavioral health services; peer support services; provision of basic necessities including food, transportation and clothing; vocational services; and mentor partnerships.

It is important to record that I am a Sister of Mercy of the Americas. Spiritual content in the book reflects my personal appropriation and integration of gospel living. It does not pretend to represent Roman Catholic teachings.

I am grateful to the many Sisters of Mercy who encouraged me to write and publish this book and the leadership of the Sisters of Mercy, South Central (now Sisters of Mercy of the Americas) who made it financially possible for me to do so.

A word about the book's name. On the last day of each month's course, *Becoming All We Can Be*, I invited the justice-involved-women to tell me one important thing they learned during the course, *Becoming All We Can Be*. One woman responded, "I learned that I am a Somebody." Thus, the title of this book. Clearly, most people have no idea that justice-involved-women have a history of childhood victimization. To make this obvious, I added the subtitle, "Emerging From the Shadows."

Finally, I feel deeply indebted to the many incarcerated women who, in the sharing of their lives, invited me into the sacred reality of Sacramental Living. They Baptized me in their tears; nourished me with the Bread and Wine of their lives; Confirmed and Ordained me with their affirmations of my gifts; and when I stumbled, Forgave me with their honesty and humor. Most especially, they allowed me to accompany them through the Suffering, Death and Resurrections in their lives. I found myself, when with them, immersed in the Communion of Saints.

I AM A SOMEBODY:
EMERGING FROM THE SHADOWS

CHAPTER 1:
TRAUMA AND RESILIENCE

In chapters two and beyond, you will read about the traumatic experiences that twisted innocent girls' self-concepts into caricatures of themselves. Often a member of the child's family perpetrated the traumas, now known as "adverse childhood experiences (ACE)." Having no one to save them, the girls tried to save themselves, using the only means available: running away, drugs, prostitution, and crime.

When police found the runaways, they returned them home where the trauma continued. Eventually, the traumatized youth reached adulthood with psychic wounds and criminal records.

But before you read their stories, let's define trauma and resilience.

TRAUMA

Trauma is exposure to actual or threatened death, serious injury, or sexual violence in one or more of four ways:

a.   directly experiencing the event;

b.   witnessing, in person, the event occurring to another;

c.   learning that such an event happened to a close family member or friend;

d.   experiencing repeated or extreme exposure to aversive details of such events, such as with first responders.

(American Psychiatric Association, *Diagnostic and Statistical Manual of Mental Disorders*, 2013).

An incarcerated woman has experienced an average of six traumatic events in her lifetime, whereas a typical woman in the community has experienced an average of two ... Incarcerated women also have higher rates of post-traumatic stress disorder (PTSD) than women in the community (40 percent versus 12 percent) and are 10 times more likely to use illegal substances in response to trauma (64 percent versus 6 percent).

(Stephanie Covington, PhD, Beyond Trauma: A Healing Journey for Women, Center City, MN. 2016).

Occasionally, people tell me they know adults with traumatized early lives who did not commit crimes. Their point, of course, is that crime is unrelated to childhood trauma. I readily acknowledge that victims do not necessarily become victimizers. However, most victimizers were first victims. Deeply rooted oak trees can stand tall against the forces of nature. But, like shallow pancake-rooted pear trees, children and teens who suffer traumas may be physically and psychically upended by those experiences.

Covington (ibid above) divides traumas into two types: public and private. Public traumas, like natural disasters, affect a large segment of a community and are highly publicized. Private traumas, including rape, incest, and domestic violence often remain concealed from the public and even from the victim's family members.

People suffering from public traumas experience pain and deprivation. But the public sympathizes with the victims and often provides physical, emotional and, sometimes, financial support for them. While public traumas are tragic and often involve long-term recovery efforts, they can also bring communities together, energizing and propelling individuals into more healthy lives.

This is rarely the case for people suffering from <u>private</u> traumas. They suffer alone, feel humiliated, and hide their pain. Sometimes others, including their families, further shame them by refusing to believe them, or by taunting them with statements such as a mother did to her daughter, Cissie, who ended up in jail: "You brought it on yourself."

In the stories that follow, each woman suffered several different kinds of trauma. But, to better highlight a single trauma in each story, I emphasize only one.

RESILIENCE

Some women overcome their trauma symptoms, and some do not. Those who do are said to be resilient. They have the ability to overcome and bounce back from personal hardships or, in the words of the American Psychological Association, they "[adapt] well in the face of adversity, trauma, tragedy, threats..."

> (Karen Revich, PhD & Andres Shatte', PhD. *The Resilience Factor: Finding Your Inner Strength and Overcoming Life's Hurdles.* Broadway Books: A Division of Random House, Oct. 2003).

Robert Kegan, PhD, Developmental Psychologist, uses the mnemonic scheme of RRR to summarize the elements of resilience: recruitability, reframing, and resolve. Recruitability refers to "the capacity to forge vital and enduring bonds with others." Reframing means "viewing the past through an alternate frame ... [it] helps us to reinterpret negative experiences." Resolve is the "determination ... to do 'whatever is necessary, no matter the defeats and bruises along the way, to overcome the adversities of life.'"

> (Robert Kegan, PhD, quoted in James and Evelyn Whitehead. *The Virtue of Resilience.* Orbis Books: Maryknoll NY, 10548, 2015).

We discuss resilience in my course, *Becoming All We Can Be*, in the jail. With help participants identify the strengths they developed as they coped with their ACE's. The purpose is to use those strengths to envision themselves not simply as survivors, but as thrivers.

I encourage them to name their own reality by reframing their situations instead of giving that authority to others. For example, society calls them "criminals," names the building in which they are housed a "jail," and dubs the space in which they live and sleep, a "cell".

In discussion, the women name themselves students, clients, or retreatants depending on whether they see themselves as needing education, health care, or spiritual enrichment. They rename the jail as college/school, clinic/spa, or retreat house and call their cell a dorm, apartment, tent in the woods, or whatever appeals to their personal interests. (They always refuse to call it "home.")

Reframing their situations energizes them to spend their time studying, resting, journaling, and helping each other instead of venting their anger, crying for their children, or feeling victimized by "the system." As they empower themselves to take control of their thoughts, attitudes, and actions, they move from obsessing about their problems to identifying and designing their own solutions.

For example, Sally, a very intelligent woman of about 30 had been arrested as a gang leader. She chose to see her future self as a teaching psychologist. She negotiated with the jail's commanding officer (CO) who allowed her to hold spelling bees for women without high school diplomas. Each day the CO provided a candy bar for the winner.

Keneisha devoted herself to learning a new word each day. She challenged and amused her peers and me with her interesting vocabulary. "Today," she might say, "I feel unexpectedly like an opportunist" or "peculiarly inquisitive." One day, toward the end of her incarceration, she said "I have a combination of ambivalence, yet certainty, about my life." A big grin followed, and I said, "Would you like to tell us more about that, Keneisha?"

"No," she answered, still smiling.

Keneisha had, in the first class, named herself **"IRATE"** because a police officer had shot and killed her dog. During our course, she edited her name card until the last day of class when it looked like "ira." The small thin letters told me that she had healed her rage.

Now to the stories of women in jail and the traumas that propelled them into crime.

CHAPTER TWO:
MIRIAM

LIVING WITH A MENTALLY UNSTABLE, MOTHER

MIRIAM'S BACKGROUND INFORMATION

Miriam's body bore a bit more weight – maybe 40 pounds – than was healthy, but that didn't seem unusual in a 50-year-old mother of two. Heavier than her physical poundage, was the load she bore in her heart.

I never saw her smile.

In our first class, I give each of the eight women a blank sheet of tri-folded paper and instruct them to print on it the name they want to be called. I suggest that they decorate this name card to tell us something about themselves: how they feel, what they like, or something about their personality.

Miriam simply printed in black M i r i a m. No color. No decorations. When she introduced herself, she simply said, "I'm a private person." In response to a homework question: Name a belief you have about yourself which may be only partially true, she wrote: "I am fat, dumb, and ugly." (You may be surprised, as you read her story, that she was actually quite intelligent.) However, her life experiences hid her brain power from her consciousness.

Over the course of nine classes, nine sets of homework and a few personal interviews, I learned that Miriam's mother, Cecile, married three times and birthed 12 children. Her (Cecile's) parents "adopted out" Cecile's first and third babies, born during her teen years. Cecile's mother and stepfather raised her second child, born during a three-months marriage.

Miriam and her sister, Diana, were Cecile's fourth and fifth children but the first to be raised by Cecile. This, of course, made Miriam the "oldest child" in the home. The two girls' birth father left this family shortly after Diana's birth. Cecile then married Harvey and had seven children with him, although the seventh died at birth.

As mentioned earlier, I have recorded most of these stories in the women's own words, without correcting their grammar.

IN MIRIAM'S WORDS

"We were very poor. Too many nights we went to bed hungry. When Harvey, Sr., a Vietnam Veteran, did work and had some money, my mom would go and buy us all kinds of toys and clothes, but we wouldn't have money, the next week, for food and electricity. I can't count the number of times mom made me call my dad and ask for the child support check early.

"We moved a lot, so I was never in one school more than two years. Sometimes we were evicted and sometimes we moved to a house that wasn't so run down. I was not very smart, and I had to repeat three grades. So, I was always older and bigger than the others in my class and they made fun of me.

"My mom was deeply troubled. She would do horrible things to us. She was physically and emotionally abusive, deceitful, and manipulative. Harvey was a spineless man who left the childcare to mom. When mom said me and Diana deserved a beating, he made us pull our pants down and lay across the bed so his belt would hit our bare skin.

"There was sexual abuse too. Mom would walk around the house naked, and Harvey would touch her in sexual ways. When my brothers were babies, she would touch their genitals with her mouth and Harvey would make lewd comments. Just remembering this makes me sick.

"I remember, at age five, being sexually abused by a male babysitter who was 14. I think Harvey knew about this because he made a comment about me being too old to be wearing just a nightgown around this boy.

"Diana and I, and sometimes Judy, slept in the back bedroom. I used to always pray that we would go to sleep and never wake up. One night when I was nine, mom told me to sleep in the front bedroom with her, Harvey, Sr., little Harvey, and baby Shelly. Mom had, never before, told me to do that, and I wondered why she did it that night. That was the night our house caught fire. Diana, Judy, and Shelly all died in that fire. I thought I caused them to die because of what I prayed for.

"Once the fire started, Harvey, Sr. saved Boyd and Teresa who were locked in another room. They were about three and four. Harvey, Sr. was badly burned and spent six months in the hospital. Mom got Harvey, Jr. and me out of the house but left Shelley, who was only one, in her crib to burn to death.

"I've always thought our mother started that fire.

"Since that fire, there's been so much that I have forgotten. My teacher told mom I needed help and I was seen by doctors a few times. Mom made me stop going before they could help me.

"I never really knew my birth dad that much. He would come by and pick me and Diana up and take us to the tavern where he drank. Then he'd drop us off by his parents. He was always cold and indifferent with us. The only loving memory I have of him is when I was about five. I was at my grandparents' (his parents) house. For some reason, they were gone but he was there. It was getting dark outside. I was scared and started crying. My dad was sleeping because he worked the night shift at the railroad station. My crying woke him up. He came into the bedroom and hugged and lovingly comforted me.

"I love that memory.

"After dad remarried, the only times I saw him were when mom made me get the child support check early. He'd be watching TV while I stood in the living room waiting for my stepmom to write the check. He died when I was 13. He had a heart attack.

"Before the fire, mom always locked Teresa, Boyd, and sometimes Judy, in a bedroom where they stayed all day. They were only allowed out to eat. It was so bad for these babies. They had no toilet, no toys, just a bed. When they went to the bathroom on the floor, they would get beat and sometimes their face would be pushed into the mess they made. Diana and I had to watch, then wash the kids up and clean the room.

"When mom and Harvey were out, Diana and I would unlock the babies' door, and play with them. Somehow though, mom and Harvey always found out about it, and Diana and I would get another beating when they got home.

"After Diana died in the fire, Suellen – she was my half-sister, mom's second child who lived with mom's parents – came to live with us and to help me with the housework.

"For some reason, mom really hated Boyd. She made up lies about him and later Harvey, Sr. verified that they were lies. For instance, mom took money from Harvey's pocket and blamed it on Boyd. She tore up papers of the other children and blamed him for it. She set little fires in the trash cans and said he did it. When he was four, Boyd threw his body through a window at home and broke his arm. Then the doctor put him in a mental hospital.

"I never had any friends after my sister, Diana, died in the fire, and I was lonely. I had a speech problem for many years, plus I was really slow in school. I was held back three times – and I was a fat kid. Being the oldest, biggest, and dumbest kid in school made me hate going. So, I quit in the 8th grade when I was about 15.

"As I got older, I started mouthing off and hitting back at mom and Harvey. I told them I would go live with my grandmother, so they backed off the beatings. They didn't want me to leave, because they would lose the railroad and the social security money we got after dad died.

"Harvey left mom when I was about 16, and they divorced after a few years. He kept in contact with us though, especially with Harvey, Jr.

"My sister, Teresa, left home when she was 14. She was one who was locked up with Boyd all those years before the fire. She came back a few times but not for long. She got into some bad stuff: drugs and sex with a lot of men – really messed up.

"I was 18 when I got pregnant by the first guy I met. We got married, and he left three months later. Our daughter, Raylene, was born when I was 19. When she was about two, I started baby-sitting three kids. I was able to bring Raylene with me and I made o.k. money. It all went for food. There were 10 of us in mom's house and the food stamps only went so far.

"In 1979 mom became sick with cancer. She died in April 1980 at the age of 46. There wasn't a time she was in the hospital that Suellen, Harvey, Jr. or I weren't with her. I would work during the day, and then spend the nights at the hospital, because she was afraid to be alone.

"This went on for four months, and in all that time she never once asked any of us to forgive her. This is so sad to me. We needed to hear that from her. I think that's why some of us have such a hard time letting go of the past.

"When I was 27, I went to get my GED. I passed and started college. I went about six months but then I quit because it was too hard to work full time, take care of the younger children and go to school. Many people do this, but I couldn't. So, I stayed in dead end jobs, just making enough to pay the bills.

"I began shoplifting when I was 13. It helped ease my depression. But then I would feel very guilty and would stop doing it for two months or so. Just stealing little things was o.k., I told myself. Over the years I started stealing more and more.

"I became a Certified Nurse Assistant (CNA) and stole Vicodin to help with my depression". (Miriam was never formally diagnosed as having depression, but a doctor did put her on Lexapro for six months.)

"I think I had maybe three dates in my whole life. One day I found this phone number for a dating phone service. I believed that was a good thing. After all, if men wanted to have sex with me, it must mean they liked me. Right? Wrong! This was how I met my son's father, Micky. He would call a couple times a week, come over for sex and then leave. I really believed that, after a while, he would come to love me. NOT!!! He took off when I became pregnant.

"The court found him, and he was ordered to pay $846/month. Micky was in the military and was going to leave the country for a few months, so I agreed for him to pay $250/month until he came back. By the time he returned he was married to someone else with a baby on the way. His wife now knows about our son, but his father, brother and his two older kids from his first marriage have no idea that our son exists.

Toward the end of the course and shortly before she was released from jail, Miriam wrote:

"I've always believed some things are not forgivable. I want to believe now, though, that God and my family whom I have embarrassed and hurt so much, can forgive me. I've been in jail since October 6. I don't know what the outcome of my trial will be, but I do know I'm not afraid anymore. I will take responsibility and deal with it the best way I can."

* * * * *

Researchers Dr. Emmy Werner and Dr. Ruth S. Smith determined that children who experienced four or more significant stressful life events were capable of resilience if one adult befriended them and if the children had the internal personality to attract an adult caretaker to them.

(Emmy E. Werner and Ruth S. Smith. *Vulnerable But Invincible: A Longitudinal Study of Resilient Children and Youth*. University of Hawaii Press, 1992.)

Miriam lacked both of those assets.

Her young life was filled with adverse childhood experiences (ACE's): poverty, frequent changes of address and schools, physical beatings, the "imprisoning" of two younger siblings by her mother, bullying by schoolmates, the fire that killed three of her siblings and for which she held herself responsible because she had prayed that she, together with them, would die, molestation by a baby sitter and, especially, the ongoing behavior of her mentally unstable mother. The one teacher who tried, after the fire, to get help for Miriam had her efforts thwarted when Miriam's mother terminated her daughter's therapy.

Beginning at age 13, Miriam made herself feel better by stealing "little things at first." Later, after her sister died and her son's father married someone else, she stole medications from her patients.

Actions like theft, prostitution, and illegal drug use which society calls crimes were actually Mary's childhood/teen coping mechanisms – attempts to gain some power over her life's traumas.

We, as a society, have not yet learned to look beneath the surface of crimes to see the traumas which triggered them. Instead of providing therapy, we imprison the traumatized women, thus further victimizing them.

Miriam, who entered jail in October 2005, grew in self-esteem and self-respect during the course, *Becoming All We Can Be*. On her final course paper, she wrote "It's o.k. to forgive myself. It's o.k. to love myself. I've become a strong, caring woman. As my daughter has told me many times, I cannot let my past dictate my future."

After serving a few months in jail, officials released Miriam on five-years-probation. With state permission she moved to Texas to be with her young son and her daughter's family. She easily found employment with a telephone company and worked hard at it until 2010 when, at the age of 54, she died. I was unable to learn the cause of her death. However, I do know that she had a cardiac disorder.

Scripture tells us that one of Jesus's last requests to his followers was "when you do this (break bread with friends) remember me." Miriam "broke and shared the bread" of her life when she shared her life story with us. Whenever I remember her, I am energized to work for restorative justice - systemic change – to help, instead of further victimizing, incarcerated women.

CHAPTER THREE:
TERRY

TRAUMA OF ABANDONMENT

"Life is full of orphaning experiences and some people have more than their share of them."

(Carol S. Pearson. *Awakening the Heroes Within*. Harper: A Division of Harper Collins Publishers. SanFrancisco, CA. 1991).

TERRY

*S*arah ejected her oldest daughter Rita Rae, a 15-year-old drug user, from the family home when Rita Rae's daughter, Terry, was born. Terry grew up thinking Sarah was her mother. She called Sarah "mom."

Besides Rita Rae, Sarah had two other daughters: Naomi and Pat. Each of them was several years older than Terry, who thought they were her sisters.

Lyle was Sarah's fifth (some sources say seventh) husband. Sarah married and divorced one husband three times so that may account for the number seven. Terry vaguely remembered the husband prior to Lyle, but Lyle was the only one she ever called "dad."

IN TERRY'S WORDS:

"It was Hallowe'en night, 1982. I remember it like it was yesterday. I was a witch for Hallowe'en that year. I had a good time trick-or-treating. I then went for a ride with my aunts Naomi and Pat. At the time I thought they were my older sisters.

"When we got back home, my grandmother whom I called mom and my step-grandfather whom I called dad, were in bed. I always went into their room and watched TV at night, but I wasn't allowed to watch TV that night. So, I kissed them both, told them I loved them and went to my room. I was eight years old. I didn't realize that life as I knew it would never be the same.

"I awoke the next morning and ate my usual breakfast of a Pepsi and a fudge sickle. As I finished my soda, mom walked out of their bedroom and woke up Naomi and Pat. Mom said we had to go to the water company immediately and pay the water bill. She stayed home and the three of us went.

"When we arrived back home, my mom told us to go into her bedroom. She had something to show us.

"Dad was dead.

"Mom had already stripped him and cleaned up his body. The most vivid thing I remember was his tongue. It was swollen, purple and out of his mouth. She said, 'Look, girls! This is what death looks like.'

"I was absolutely devastated. The only man I had ever called dad, the only man that I ever loved, was gone. I only had him for a little more than a year and he was gone. He was my best friend. He taught me. He nurtured me. He loved me, and now he was gone.

"I went with mom to the funeral home, and I picked out his casket – powder blue – his favorite color. It had a plaque of the Last Supper on the inside of the top. He was studying to be Catholic so he could be closer to us. Mom had the funeral and burial very quickly.

"On November 6, Naomi called the police and the next thing I knew, she and I were in a police car on our way to the police station. Mom and Pat were out Christmas shopping. At the police station, Naomi went into a room with one officer, and I was left with another. He asked me if I had eaten dinner and I told him that I hadn't. He brought me a carton of milk and a bologna sandwich. Later the officers drove us home. I thought they had left. I turned on the TV and waited for mom to get home.

"When she pulled into the driveway, she and Pat grabbed the shopping bags and came inside. In a flash police kicked down the door and tackled mom. She kept saying that she had to use the bathroom. They let her go to the bathroom. When she came out, they threw her on the floor and cuffed her, all of this in front of me. I was so scared for her. Why were they doing this? Why did I have to witness it?'

"Mom's lawyer came to pick up Naomi and Pat and me. We spent a week or two with him and his family. That was when everything hit the news and the papers. I would watch the 10 pm news so I could say 'goodnight' to my mom. I cried a lot.

"After that, Naomi went to live with her boyfriend. Pat and I went to live with one of mom's sisters and her husband. They had four kids. I had been the baby at home and now I was an outsider. Three of the four children made fun of me and said hateful things about mom. My aunt and uncle didn't seem to care. I was miserable. Absolutely miserable.

"I went back to catholic school but only lasted a few days before I kicked a nun and called her a bitch. Expelled – never to attend another catholic school. I am on the catholic school blacklist.

"Then they put me into a public school. My first day I fought the principal. She wrapped me in her arms instead of fighting my fists. She locked herself in a bathroom with me for a whole day. She listened to me and let me cry. Later in my time at that school she and I were close. I love that woman.

"One night I woke up to my uncle on top of me, kissing me and putting himself inside of me. That was the beginning of four years of hell. I just lost my mom and dad and now he was doing this.

"At age 13 I tried to commit suicide. My aunt walked into the room and found me with a gun to my head. She took me to the psychiatric hospital. I told her what her husband had been doing to me. She called me a liar. The doctors checked me and said I had told the truth. They let me out of the hospital after that. I was sane – just very hurt and confused.

"My aunt divorced my uncle and we moved two blocks away. Every day my aunt told me it was my fault she was divorced.

"I buried myself in school, sports, clubs – the whole nine yards. When my aunt's boyfriend would come over, she would hand me a $20 bill and tell me to leave for a couple of hours. I would walk to the 7-11 and play pinball. As the years passed, I made some friends and started spending the money on cigarettes, alcohol, and pot.

"When I was 16, my aunt put me into an adolescent group home. She told them I was a drug addict and crazy. I stayed there nine days. I was still very sane. Just more hurt and even more confused.

"Backtrack: age 13. I found my biological mother, Rita Rae. She was mom's oldest daughter. I learned that mom put her out of the house when I was born. I began a relationship with her. A guy at school gave me a joint (marijuana) and I got really sick. Come to find out, it was laced with heroin. I told Rita Rae about it. That's when she started giving me weed. She said 'at least if I give it to you, I know you're not getting something that's gonna' kill you or something...'

"Rita Rae was great. I snuck around to see her every chance I got. I had to sneak these visits because my aunt wouldn't allow me to see her otherwise. She called Rita Rae an addict and a whore. I didn't care what my aunt said. Rita Rae was my mother and I wanted to see her.

"In January of my senior year I moved in with Rita Rae and quit school. I tried to go back to school on two different occasions but that didn't work. I was too involved in drugs. I went, about a year ago, down to a center in Wellston and took the GED pre-test. They told me I didn't have to take any classes – to just go and take the test. I didn't do that, but I hope to get my GED while I'm here in jail.

"I had always lived in nice houses in the county. The people I knew there never stole cars or robbed houses. The only laws we broke were the alcohol and drug laws. Rita Rae lived in the city. Boy, was I in a whole new world! I started tripping acid (an hallucinogenic drug like LSD), stealing car stereos, and robbing houses. It was just a downward spiral, and I thought that if I moved out of Rita Rae's house, I would be better.

"I knew I was lesbian from my early years. Sometime after I moved out of Rita Rae's apartment, I moved in with a girlfriend and it was better in one way, but I let her control me. She was physically abusive during the first two years we lived together, but she stopped that. We smoked crack together for a while, but we eventually quit and were clean for five years before I started using again this last time.

"I wanted a baby and while we were clean my partner had a baby for us. I loved that little girl and the three of us had a wonderful life for a while, but my partner and I are no longer together.

"I fell back into the lifestyle I had left. Crack cocaine is a very powerful drug. It can turn me into the worst person in the world. My partner was still doing pot (marijuana) but couldn't tolerate my crack-filled behavior. She kicked me out of the house and wouldn't let me have any contact with our little girl. Eventually police arrested me.

"Today I'm 31 and in jail for burglary. I was smoking crack but have now been clean for 33 days. I have found God and I am thankful that He took me out of the situation I was in. I hope that, someday, I will be reunited with my partner and my little girl."

* * * * *

Terry had more than her share of abandonment. When we consider the fact that abandonment leaves us feeling orphaned, Terry was orphaned

– either physically, emotionally, or spiritually – by almost everyone, albeit unintentionally, in her circle of acquaintances.

She was abandoned by:

- Rita Rae, her birth mother, whom Sarah ejected from her home,
- her stepfather, Lyle, "the only dad I ever knew," when he died,
- Sarah, the grandmother, when she was imprisoned,
- her uncle who incested her,
- her aunt who punished Terry for reporting the incest,
- the catholic school nun who, whether aware of Terry's painful situation or not, failed to understand that the nine-year-old orphaned child's unruly behavior was an acting out of grief,
- her aunts, Naomi and Pat, who drifted out of Terry's life when they could legally do so,
- her partner, Mel, who evicted Terry from her life, and the life of their child.

Finally, it must be said that Terry abandoned herself to drugs and the crimes that her addictions spawned.

Though not essential to this story, the reader may feel incomplete without follow-up about Sarah. Newspaper accounts, following Lyle's death and Sarah's imprisonment, reported that Lyle's body was "saturated with ethylene glycol, an ingredient in antifreeze." The body of a previous husband was exhumed and he, too, was found to have been poisoned. A third husband said he thought Sarah had tried to kill him too, but he left her before she put enough poison into his body.

Authorities found several different ID's in Sarah's possession. She claimed to be a registered nurse and worked in a doctor's office but had never attended a school of nursing. While imprisoned, she claimed to be pregnant with twins, although she had had a hysterectomy many years previously. Prison doctors diagnosed her as having paranoid schizophrenia.

In an interview with Terry after she submitted her story, I asked if, looking back now on her childhood, she recognized signs of mental illness in Sarah.

At age seven, Terry told me, "I smoked a cigarette butt. Mom caught me and made me eat a bunch of cigarettes. She kept a ball bat and a can of bug spray in very room of the house. I was just a kid then, and I thought every house was like that."

When Sarah was 42, a judge sentenced her to 50 years in prison without the possibility of probation or parole. She died in prison.

Terry spent 30 months in prison. At the time of this writing, she has been free and gainfully employed for several years. A newspaper article, which cited Terry's post-imprisonment story, noted that she was been reunited with her much- loved daughter. The article did not mention Terry's partner. It added that Terry is a strong advocate for animals and for the Lesbian gay, bi-sexual and transgendered community. Apparently, she has transformed the pain of her abandonment into a strength that energizes her to rescue others: people and animals, who have been abandoned.

CHAPTER FOUR:
LIVING IN A DYSFUNCTIONAL FAMILY

JUDY

*J*udy was born into a blended family. Her mother, Evelyn, had three sons: Ron, Dirk and Leonard from a previous marriage. Judy's father, Les, had a son, John, and a daughter, Tara, from an earlier marriage. Judy, the only child of Evelyn and Les, was 25 when I met her. She chose to tell her story verbally instead of writing it.

IN JUDY'S WORDS

"Both of my parents used drugs. Their relationship was abusive. When I was four, a judge sentenced my half-brother, Ron, to ten years in prison for armed robbery. Before I was born, Dirk served four years in prison and when I was seven, he went to prison for seven more years. At the current time, he is serving a twenty-year sentence for additional crimes."

Judy did not mention her half-brothers, Leonard and John. My sense is that they lived either alone or with their other parents. Whatever their circumstances, they seemed not to people Judy's life.

"Mom stopped using drugs when I was 12 or 13, and left dad. I had no idea that she was unhappy in their marriage. I thought every couple's relationship was abusive.

"I blamed mom for leaving and, although she wanted me to go with her, I stayed with dad. I enjoyed school, but dad allowed me to stay home whenever I wanted.

"On weekends, beginning when I was 14, my friends spent time at our house. Dad supplied us with alcohol and marijuana. In that same year, Ron and Dirk came home from prison and lived with us. My half-sister, Tara, died of AIDS which she contracted from her boyfriend, the father of her two-year-old baby. Tara's mother raised her baby.

"At age 15 I met a guy I liked and went to live with him. The next year I dropped out of school and got my GED. My baby girl was born when I was 17. She is now eight. When our baby was two-months old, my boyfriend was sent to prison. He has been in and out of prison for the entire 10 years we have lived together.

"When I was 19, I started snorting cocaine, and forged checks to pay for the drugs. At age 20, I left my boyfriend.

"Dad died of an overdose when I was 23. That was very hard on me. In the meantime, mom married three different times after divorcing dad. She is currently in a stable, non-abusive relationship with a very nice guy. She has been drug-free for 19 years.

"Mom and her husband want to adopt my little girl because they are financially stable, and I am not. They have offered to buy a trailer for me, and place it on their property, so I can be near my daughter and have my own space. I would like that."

* * * * *

It is hard to get one's head around the traumas and instabilities in Judy's life. Her teen and young-adult years remind me of a boat tossed against stones in a stormy sea:

- her parents' drug-use and divorce,
- the crimes and imprisonment of her stepbrothers,

- the addition of her two half-brothers to the father's home, and the death of her stepsister,
- her mother's additional three marriages, prior to her drug-free marriage,
- Judy becoming a school drop-out, and leaving her father's home to live with her boyfriend,
- the birth of her child,
- her boyfriend's 10-year cycle in and out of incarceration,
- Judy's crack cocaine habit,
- the death of her father when she was 23.

Judy had few, if any, mature adults to ground her childhood/teen years. When she was 12 or 13, living with her father, her mother stopped using drugs and married three more times before entering a stable marital relationship.

The Weber research on resilience indicated that a stable caring relationship was a strength in helping children overcome four or more traumatic life events. Judy left her boyfriend (who was in prison) when she was 20. Her father overdosed when she was 23.

Perhaps her mother's eventual drug-free marital relation provided some stability for her. At least we know that her mother and stepfather tried to help Judy by adopting her baby and offering a trailer on their property once Judy was out of jail.

Judy was 25 when I met her. At the time of this story, she is 39. Following her release from jail she was arrested two additional times for possession of a controlled substance (marijuana). She is currently on probation.

During her formative years, both of Judy's parents were unstable drug-addicted adults. Her father died in an overdose, while her mother eventually moved into a stable, healthy relationship. In my last encounter with Judy, her life hovered toward the healthiness of her mother. My hope is that she is now enjoying a healthy, happy life.

CHAPTER FIVE:
SUBSTANCE ABUSE DISORDER

*A*s mentioned before, most of the women I encountered in jail had a substance abuse disorder. However, I focused on stories related to other problems in their lives – problems which propelled them into unhealthy relationships, drugs, and crime. I have chosen to focus this chapter on drugs themselves. Following it, I will share stories about a woman who was born to a drug-addicted mother; a woman who self-medicated to relieve her emotional imbalance; and a woman drug-dealer.

Research shows that excessive alcohol use poses more threats to women than to men.

ALCOHOL:

> Although men are more likely to drink alcohol and drink in larger amounts, gender differences in body structure and chemistry cause women to absorb more alcohol, and take longer to break it down and remove it from their bodies (i.e. to metabolize it). In other words, upon drinking equal amounts, women have higher alcohol levels in their blood than men, and the immediate effects of alcohol occur more quickly and last longer in women than men.

> (Ashley MJ et al, *Morbidity in Alcoholics, Evidence for Accelerated Development of Physical Disease in Women.* [http://www.ncbi.nlm.nih.gov/pubmed/8799277?dopt=Abstract] reported in Centers for Disease Control and Prevention Fact Sheets – Excessive Alcohol Use and Risks to Women's Health).

The Centers for Disease Control and Prevention (CDCP) has long cautioned women against excessive alcohol intake, reporting that women have a higher risk than men of liver disease, shrinkage of the brain tissue, damage to the heart muscle, and breast cancer. In addition, the CDCP has strongly cautioned pregnant and lactating women against drinking, because alcohol passes directly into the woman's umbilical cord, thus into the fetus and breast milk. It can cause a series of developmental problems for babies, and those problems are not reversible.

> Alcohol interferes with the delivery of oxygen and optimal nutrition to your developing baby … Fetal alcohol syndrome causes brain damage and growth problems. The problems caused by fetal alcohol syndrome vary from child to child, but defects caused by fetal alcohol syndrome are not reversible … [They] may include … small head circumference and brain size … intellectual disability, learning disorders … poor social skills … problems with behavior and impulse control…
>
> (Mayo Foundation for Medical Education and Research [MF-MER] Mayo Clinic Patient Care & Health Information: Fetal Alcohol Syndrome 1998-2019).

ILLEGAL DRUGS:

Women, themselves, report unique reasons for using drugs.

> [These include] controlling weight, fighting exhaustion, coping with pain, and self-treating mental health problems … 15.8 million women (or 12.9 percent) ages 18 or older have used illicit drugs in the past year.
>
> (Substance Abuse and Mental Health Services Administration [SAMSA] Results from the 2013 National Survey on Drug Use and Health: Summary of National Findings. Rockville MD, 2014.HHS Publication No. 14-4863).

Once they begin using alcohol and illegal drugs, women continue using these substances for a variety of reasons. Of the eight women who enrolled in my monthly course at the jail, an average of seven have addictions either to alcohol, heroin, methamphetamines, cocaine, prescription medications or a combination of these drugs. Many also admit to the use of marijuana but none in 27 years has indicated a marijuana addiction.

The women's reasons for using alcohol and/or illegal drugs vary:

1) failure to fit into family or peer groups: "I didn't make it to college, but I added a room to my parents' home – did all of the carpentry, electrical and plumbing work myself," 45 year old Ellie said. However, that giftedness did not overcome her feelings that she is a misfit among her highly educated parents and siblings. Police arrested her seven times for DUI. Still, she reported that her affluent, civic-minded parents deny that she has alcoholism. They dissuade her from drug rehab and AA meetings because "we're not alcoholics like those people."

2) to cope with life's challenges: Stefania, a talented singer, wife and mother of three, first tried drugs at a neighborhood women's party. The drugs allowed her to face the fact that she is lesbian. When she told her husband, he took the children and left her. She drugs to cope with her grief.

3) to self-medicate: Margie's doctor prescribed an opioid for the back pain which followed an accident. Addiction followed. Police arrested her when she forged her physician's name on prescription pads stolen from his office. Norma had the same back problem but easily found heroin in her neighborhood. Police arrested her for stealing to feed her addiction.

4) trapped with a drug-dealing spouse: Faith was the only woman who came to class one day. A tall, thin woman of about 45, she was soon to be released and worried that she would return to drugs once she arrived home. In her limited language, she told me "husband's a dealer. I'se a addict. Stay with him, stay on drugs. Leave him, burn in hell. No way out."

Fortunately, a conversation about her harsh understanding of her religion's teachings about God, convinced her that leaving her husband was a viable way out of her dilemma.

5.) To numb pain. Seven of every eight women in my classes experienced incest as children. Drugs numb their painful feelings surrounding these experiences.

To deny that drug addiction is a problem in our society is to bury one's head in the sand. Finding a viable solution, however, has eluded legislators.

Instead of uncovering the causes, they direct their attention to supply and demand: cut off the supply – make the drugs unavailable and lock up the users.

This approach seems similar to an exterminator who, after removing squirrels from a homeowner's attic, saws off the tree limb that gives the squirrel access to the house. This "solution" fails to appreciate squirrel ingenuity. Nor does it examine the ecological reasons behind the glut of squirrels in the neighborhood.

Legislators fail to acknowledge and internalize the fact, announced by the American Medical Association as long ago as 1956, that addictions are illnesses, not moral failures.

Barbara Baker, who serves as Advocacy Director for the Center for Women in Transition in St. Louis, spent more than 15 years in prison for crimes related to her heroin addiction. As a young teen, she and her friends spent weekends "tripping" on Robitussin with Codeine. In those days, Robitussin with Codeine was an inexpensive over-the-counter cough medicine. Once legislators became aware that teens used it "to get high," they placed cough medicine on prescription status.

With the codeine product no longer available over the counter, Barbara and her teen friends turned to heroin which produced effects similar to codeine. Unfortunately, heroin is more potent than codeine. Additionally, pharmacological industries strictly measured the amount of codeine in the cough medicine, while the amounts of opium vary in heroin. As a result, large numbers of young people became heroin dependent.

The stories that follow feature Carrie, Melissa and Shelana, justice-involved-women with drug-addiction disorders.

CHAPTER SIX:
CARRIE

BORN TO AN ADDICTED MOTHER

IN CARRIE'S WORDS

"*I* was born to a 16-year-old drug addict whose mental health problems included paranoid schizophrenia and bi-polar disorder. And she has the mental capacity of a 12-year-old. I don't know if she always had these problems or if they resulted from her abuse of alcohol and illegal drugs.

"Mom said her parents begged her to get an abortion when she was pregnant with me but, to spite them, she refused. My birth father's family moved to another state to escape my birth, or so, mom said. I know his name, but I've never met him.

"Mom said she was a full-blown alcoholic and on PCP (Phencyclidine – a mind-altering drug known, on the streets, as 'angel dust') when she was pregnant with me. At any rate, I tested positive for drugs at one day old, so I guess you could say I was born to get high!

"Because mom was in jail when I was born, I was taken from the delivery room to the Department of Family Services (DFS) and then fostered out to a couple who were friends of the family. I can't remember much until the following first memory of my mom.

"I was five years old, and I thought my foster parents were my parents. They are dead now and I only have pictures of them. I remember feeling loved by them. That would soon change.

"The cops came and took me forcefully out of the house. I remember saying 'help, mommy and daddy.' They tried. They got arrested for resisting police, and I was placed in the arms of a bald lady. The cop said, 'This is your mom.'

"'What?' I could say nothing else. I was so, so, so, confused.

"I found out later that mom was bald because she had just been released from a mental hospital where she received shock therapy. In the process they shaved her head.

"This bald lady took me to her one-bedroom house. I remember thinking, 'wow! How small.' And I felt so out of place.

"There was an old man lying on the couch. He was high on pot then and always. He was my mom's husband and was 15 years older than she was. He said, 'Hi. Come here.' "I did. I've, since then, tried to block every memory of him out of my head – all the horrible nights – and baths – all of it. I would be blocking it out for the next 14 years – that's how long she stayed with him.

"But lucky me. A few years later my mother took me to a dope house in the city. Me and two other kids there, decided to take a walk down the highway. Cops picked us up and took me to the Department of Family Services (DFS).

"The next family I was placed with had to be the weirdest. One day me and a boy who lived with them, ate a bag of marshmallows. The couple caught us, took us into a room, stripped us naked and beat us. I don't remember if it hurt. All I remember is I did NOT want to be naked ever again.

"For some reason I was taken from that home and placed with my maternal grandma. She told me that I ruined my mother's life. I was the reason mom used drugs. I was responsible for mom's craziness. I was even the reason mom couldn't find God. My grandma was convinced I was straight from Satan.

"I guess grandma eventually had enough (of me) and I went to live with my Aunt Lorene and her husband. Wow! This lady loved me. How strange, I thought. Why is she so nice and so beautiful? I never wanted to leave.

"Only one problem here. This husband of hers drank and beat her. I hated that. Why would he do that to her? If I broke something or did something wrong, she told him it was her fault. She was my angel. I prayed he would leave or die. Then one day, while me and my cousin who was three or four years old watched, he shot himself in the head with a shotgun. I was seven years old, and I thought I had killed him – my little cousin's daddy.

"In the meantime, my mom's HOT! She hates this sister of hers – can't understand why I don't want to leave Aunt Lorene and go back home. She believed Aunt Lorene brainwashed my head.

"Sometime after that, Aunt Lorene marries a good man who has two sons. Problem is they live in a two-bedroom house and DFS requires a separate third bedroom for me. So, I have to return to mom.

"My step-grandpa moves next door to mom. He and my stepfather like to photograph people naked – especially me. The next five years went just like this: stepdad and step-grandpa would sexually abuse me. It hurt me in more ways than one. They took from me something I can never get back. My mom would, in turn, beat my ass and then get upset and take off with me.

"She would leave me for days with men she was getting high with. Many times, I would just get up and leave. The police would pick me up while I was walking – I guess because I was only seven or eight or younger – and take me to DFS. They would call my grandpa or aunt and send me home with them. But then, my mom would get 'clean' of drugs, and she would take me back to my stepdad's and the process would repeat itself.

"The sexual abuse eased up as I got older, and my mom started beating my ass for different reasons – like taking all her medications. My stepdad had given me mom's meds before the sexual encounters, and I took them because they helped me not remember. I liked the pills so I would tell everyone who wanted to know that I wasn't being abused.

"We must have moved 12 times before I was in middle school: St. Charles, Wentzville, Maryland Heights, St. Ann's, Bridgeton, Woodson Terrace (all in St. Louis County MO) in about three or four different school districts. We moved so much because, when my mom smokes crack and has sex with all the neighbors, it's time to move.

"In school we had this program about drugs. I came straight home to let my stepdad know that selling weed (marijuana) was illegal. He beat my ass good for that. The next day the officer said, 'if your mom or dad uses drugs, they will surely die.' That was the best news I had ever heard. I couldn't wait. But they didn't die, and, at a young age, drugs were on for me. By age 13, I was using as much drugs as the adults around me.

"I had no friends, and we had no money – shopped at Good Will. My stepdad had seven kids with grandkids, so his money was in them – not me. I learned to steal – my first addiction.

"We lived four blocks from the mall and across the street from WalMart. How easy. Now I'm cool at school. I've got the best of everything. My mom and stepdad never knew until I got caught with two large Famous-Barr bags – FULL – over $2,000 worth of clothes and stuff.

"Finally, the Department of Juvenile Offenders (DJO) says 'enough stealing and running away. You're going to Lakeside' – one of the homes for kids who are bad. Only BAD kids get beat. Right? If I'd been a good kid, none of that would have happened.

"My grades dropped from A's to C's. I missed lots of school, ran away from home, stole a car, stole from stores and from my family. It was cars, cash and drugs all day and night. My life was out of control. I was 14. No one paid much attention to me but the cops. No one ever said I was an addict. I was suspended from the eighth grade for 'breaking and entering'.

"Another girl and I ran away from one of the juvenile homes. She was 14 and I was 15. With a sheet of acid (LSD) and a bunch of meth, we went to a truck stop and hitchhiked to California.

"We called Lakeside to let them know we were o.k., and that's when the s—t hit the fan. That trucker had us back in St. Louis in, like, no time.

"At age 16, I tried heroin for the first time with my aunt. It was also the first time I shot (injected) dope. I loved it.

"Shortly afterwards, I met Ronnie. He taught me everything I never needed to know. He was 26 and I was 16. He sold just about everything, and I used it.

"The next five to six years were full of bruises and heartache. But I could handle it. I had licked bruises and heartache years earlier. No problem. Plus, now, with his drug money, I had it all: a house, two cars in my name. I was finishing school and I had an unlimited supply of whatever drug I wanted. I was Ronnie's girl and everybody knew it.

"Ronnie loved to box – mostly on me. He loved to f—k all of my 'friends.' And I was totally in love?? with him.

"In the next five years I had one abortion, one miscarriage and numerous trips to the E.R. for 'falling down the stairs.'

"We lived in Arkansas for the last three of those years. It was there that I decided I had had enough. I just woke up one day, packed all of my s—t in my truck and told Ronnie I had had it. I was off of heroin and cocaine at that time but using Mary Janes (marijuana) and meth practically daily.

"I remember telling God that Ronnie was eventually going to kill me and that I needed to get out. I went outside to find that Ronnie had set my truck on fire with everything I owned inside it. He looked at me and said, 'you can leave. Now!'

"So, I ran. I phoned Ronnie's friend, Bruce, to come get me. He did. And on our way back to St. Louis we made baby number one, Tessa, although I didn't know it at the time. Bruce is a wonderful man, but I was out of control. I was abusive to him. I cheated on him. And I, again, started using heroin every day.

"When I found out I was pregnant, it was like someone hit me with a two by four. I remember thinking I had to do something for real. So, I checked into a Drug Rehab Center in St. Louis for the first time. I really liked this treatment center and, after 30 days, I thought my drug problems were over. I went back to work as a shipping and receiving manager for a department store.

"After some time on this job, they fired me – and I got high. Crap!

"So, I called the rehab center. This was obviously all their fault. They must have forgotten to teach me something. They told me a place to go in Iowa – the House of Mercy for pregnant mothers. So, I went – and found myself miles away from home, in a biker town full of meth heads. I was so scared that I never left the Home.

"At nine months of my pregnancy, a few weeks before I had my baby, I called my grandpa and he sent me a greyhound ticket. I moved in with him, an alcoholic. I hated alcohol so I was safe there – or so I thought.

"Two weeks after Tessa was born, I started smoking weed, and two weeks after that I was back on heroin, and running around with another guy, Rudy.

"At the same time, me and Bruce tried to make it work for our daughter and made baby number two, my son, Micah. But how could Bruce and I make it? I was up to the same old crap: lying, cheating, stealing and shooting dope with Rudy.

"Then one night I got a call from Rudy's brother. The cops killed Rudy. I was supposed to be with Rudy that night. We were doing lots of home invasions and robberies – for heroin money. I always wonder about whether, if I had been with him, would he still be alive? Would I be dead?

"That was the first time I was, like, whoa! Everyone around me had been going to jail and now one was dead. I had to make a change. I didn't want to live like this. So, stupidly, I moved back in with my Aunt Katie.

"One day I took Katie to get some dope. When we were two houses away from home, a cop pulled us over. Tessa, about six months old, was in the back seat. I prayed that God would lock me up forever. I looked at Tessa and saw myself. I had become my mom. I hated myself and wanted to die. How could I do this to Tessa?

"While I was in jail, Micah was born. Not one person in my family would come to get him from the jail. Bruce's mother had taken Tessa when I went to jail, so I begged her to take Micah too. She said 'yes' but with conditions. I had to sign over all rights. So, I did.

"I was o.k. with this. I had been clean for the months I was in jail, and I thought I was off drugs for good. My mom's ex-boyfriend – she was no longer married to my step-father – bonded me out of jail for $10,000 cash only. No big deal, I thought. I would go to court, get probation, and he would get the bond money back.

"Only I wasn't o.k. I was still an addict. I went straight into drug rehab. This time I was going to get it right. But two days before graduating from rehab, I ran. I used drugs most of the time I was in rehab and not working on my problems. Now I was on the run and not going to court, using, and breaking the law daily.

"The cops finally caught me and, instead of probation, they sent my ass to prison.

"Looking back on that relapse, I had lost my daughter and son to Bruce's mom. Legal problems were stacking up. And I didn't care. I was going to keep drugging until it killed me.

"Prison was a bowl of cherries. About 2,000 women were housed there and I knew half of them. I did my time and got out. After release they sent me to the St. Louis Community Release Center (Honor Center) to get a job.

"I thought I had life figured out. I had x'd God out of my life. I went to meetings, had a sponsor, worked the 12 steps, while I sold weed out of the Honor Center. This is where God shows me what's what.

"I picked Al, the dumbest, brokest joker at the Honor Center, and got pregnant with my last son, Drew. I didn't use drugs – just sold them. Soon I was released from the Honor Center, had a job at Union Station, my own apartment, a car, and Al. I paid for everything myself. Al just got high. Ten days before my maternity due date, I snorted six to ten pills. (I'm not sure which). Drew was born that day.

"What was I thinking? I was 26 and getting ready to lose it all again. I broke down. This time I got on my knees and prayed that God would get me away from myself. I was the one to blame this time.

"My son was positive for heroin. The DFS took Drew, and my parole officer (PO) had no clue what to do with me. I had been dropping clean (required urine tests during visits to her PO) and was in outpatient treatment. She decided to put me in drug rehab again.

"I took a bunch of drugs to treatment with me. Ten days later I was dope sick. Mentally I felt like the world's dumbest loser. Who lives like this? Instead of staying in rehab and getting clean, I chose to get high. Then I ran – again. I didn't check in with my PO, and I didn't go to Family Drug Court - a requirement to get my son, Drew, back.

"The next two months a spiritual fight went on in my soul. I saw my aunt overdose (OD) and my friend OD'd in my apartment. I lost the car, the apartment, and my job. I had stolen some checks from my grandpa, so I was no longer welcome there.

"I took a cab to St. Louis County Jail and turned myself in. I knew that I needed help and the help had to come from God. I was the one messing up my life – not my mom, my aunt, my grandpa, nor God.

"I stayed in jail a few months, did a 120-day behavior modification program and was, then, sent back to prison.

(Carrie wrote me the following from prison.)

"Now, after more than a year in prison, I will soon be released. While here, I have studied several self-help books, and have graduated Basic Electricity

(400 hours) with a 97.1 GPA. I just hope that, now, I can get it right and get my crap together.

"Please keep praying for me. All I want is to stay clean and sober. And I want that my children never know this pain of drugs. I pray that, wherever my children are, they are safe and happy, and that I will see them again one day.

"When I get out, I will volunteer to tell young girls about my life so that they won't get caught up in drugs like me.

* * * * *

Carrie is a very intelligent young woman. While in jail, she read many self-help books. Her responses to class questions made it obvious that she understood and integrated what she learned. In addition, she has great artistic ability. Her comedic sketches remind me of the work of artists in New Orleans' French Quarter.

She is a self-motivated, empathic woman. In prison she organized other incarcerated women and facilitated discussions of books centered on personal growth. I found her to be very honest. It was Carrie who taught me that women with addictions buy (for $1.00 each) test tubes of animal urine which they insert into their vaginas prior to visiting a PO. When the PO sends them with a test tube into a bathroom, the women simply empty the animal urine into the clean test tube and return it, instead of their own urine, to the PO. (Urine tests look for evidence of drugs. They do not determine if the urine is human). Carrie told her PO about this and insisted that the PO go into the bathroom with her to make certain she was using her own urine.

Drug rehab programs differ in intensity and purpose. Some merely detoxify the user and send her on her way. Some programs are longer: 30, 60, 120 days, a year. Some are in-patient and some treat addictions on an out-patient basis. Some have follow-up-programs and some do not.

Drug programs differ in other ways too. Most include the 12-step process common to Alcoholics Anonymous. Some do not. Some center on behavior modification (the way we think, the way we handle our feelings, our patterns of association, etc.) or, as many say, "change your people, places and things."

Some programs provide information related to specific drugs: their pharmacological effects on the brain and other body organs. A few provide time and resources to address the needs of the whole person – they attend to the person's psycho-social development, the traumas a drug-user has experienced and the healing of those traumas.

Most of these latter programs, though, are out of the affordability range of all except wealthy families.

I wonder why legislators consistently focus on eliminating the supply and demand for drugs, when they can see that it doesn't eliminate our nation's drug problems. Another question is relevant here too. Why do we, the people, continue to allow legislators to use our tax monies to build prisons which have minimal resources to deal with addictions, instead of using those monies for high quality mental health facilities, which could effectively address the underlying traumas which feed the addictions?

Is not this substitution of imprisonment for therapy simply another example of legislators repeating the same behaviors and expecting different results?

But back to Carrie. She served at least one more prison sentence after writing her story for me. At the time of this writing, she has been out of prison and probation-free for over a year.

CHAPTER SEVEN:
MELISSA

SELF-MEDICATING TO RELIEVE PAIN AND EMOTIONAL
IMBALANCE

Melissa, the fourth of five siblings, was 41 years old when I met her in jail. Her oldest sibling, 11 years older than Melissa, fell out of a second-floor window before Melissa was born. She, according to Melissa, "has a steel plate in her head...and (she's) mentally challenged, kind of ..."

The second and third oldest children are male. Melissa is 10 months older than her younger sister. Melissa and her younger sister share the same parents. However, the older three children do not. Their parents were each divorced and remarried twice before Melissa's birth.

In classes, I found Melissa to be intelligent with well-developed verbal skills but lacking in spelling and writing skills. For example, she wrote "isteem" for "esteem" and "bresfast" for "breakfast." She chose to verbalize her story to me instead of writing it.

IN MELISSA'S WORDS

"We grew up in a rich neighborhood, but we were poor. I didn't know we were poor until I hit sixth grade. We were rich in spirit. We had lots of laughter in our house.

"When I was in sixth grade, I wanted a pair of Nike shoes 'cause all the other kids had them. They cost $40. So, I went to my mom, and she said 'there's no way I'm gonna' pay $40, so I went cryin' to my grandma.

"She lived three blocks away. I remember my grandma telling me 'I cried because I had no shoes, 'til I saw a man who had no feet.'

"Til I was an adult, I really didn't understand that. At the time it only made me mad, you know, (laughs)...because I wanted my Nike shoes. Later, I recognized that we lived in a rich neighborhood, but we were poor.'

"I think we had a pretty decent childhood. Now, if you ask my younger sister, she'll tell you something different, you know. Like one time I went to a psychiatrist with her because she asked me to, and she started talking about her childhood and I was like 'oh my god, we must have grown up in two different houses,' you know, but I'm the addict, probably the only addict in our family.

"I don't get that, but I'm the only one in trouble. I'm like the black sheep. But I'm not a black sheep, because I'm my dad's favorite – 'daddy's little girl'. Mom and I are close but we're so close that it makes us distant. I hurt her when I don't mean to. That's what I think.

"My older brothers and sister had a different life than I did. They lived through two divorces.

"My oldest sister fell out of a two-story window and cracked her head open. She has a steel plate in her head. She's mentally challenged, kind of. So, my oldest brother, who was close to her (oldest sister's) age, got shipped to grandma's for a long time, and I think he's angry.

"By the time it came to me and my little sister, they (parents) had been through so much. I think parenting is like everything else. The more you do it, the better you get at it.

"I knew that my mom scrubbed toilets so that we could go to Job's Daughters. She cleaned houses for extra money so that we could join dance class. My sister looked at it like they (parents) were always shipping us off somewhere. I look at it like they kept us busy and out of trouble.

"Mom was 36-37 when I was born, and 37-38 when my little sister came. My little sister was premature, so I was a baby for only a short time. I don't remember ever feeling unloved by my parents. I can remember not liking my little sister but, of course, we all feel that way sometimes.

"My younger sister and I are exact opposites. She is very judgmental, square, serious and always has something wrong with her – a hypochondriac - and always wants attention. I'm not judgmental. I'm a party girl with a lighter approach to life, and I try to push attention away from me.

In response to my question, "When did your drug problems begin?" Melissa said: "I've been an addict my whole life. Even as a child, if I liked something, I liked it to an extreme: Kool Aid, for example, and if I liked a certain kind of candy, I had to have that candy. Then men came along, and I got addicted to men – to the man of my life. I would make him my god. And to this day, I struggle with that problem.

"I often think about when St. Paul said: 'if you're married, then you worry about making your wife happy, when it would be better to be married to God and to worry about making God happy'. I think about that a lot.

"I was a good teenager. When my sister was out smoking pot, doing all that bad stuff, I wasn't. I was high on God. My sister was a beautiful girl, very popular in high school. She did all that wild stuff early on. She got pregnant at 17, married at 18, divorced at 20. I was an ugly teenager, for real. I was still a virgin when she was having sex. Now, because she went through that at a young age, by the time she was 23, she pretty much had her life together.

"I, on the other hand, started doing drugs when I was 25, 26. And I think I used – to cover up pain – because I don't like to feel (eyes mist, voice cracks). I'm full of feelings. Sometimes I feel more than I wish I did. Here's a for-instance. My son and I drove down the street right before I came in here (jail). There was this black lady on the side of the road. She had a child on one hand and one in her arms and she was crying – just sobbing, and I don't know why but I just started crying. It was almost like I could feel her pain. And I don't like it. I don't want to feel hurt. I think I use drugs to cover up my feelings.

"When I got married at 27, I was a bartender. I had my own place, and I thought my life was together, but I was kind of a little out of control in the drug thing – and I got pregnant. When I got pregnant, I checked myself into

Queen of Peace (drug rehab) for 90 days. That was a big deal. I was 29, first time I ever went to rehab. I couldn't quit using drugs just because I was pregnant, so I would go home and cry to my husband and he would tell me everything was gonna' be all right. Well, I was scared to death something was gonna' happen to my child, for real. So, I just drove myself down to Queen of Peace for 90 days, lost my job of five years, lost respect of a lot of people. But I saved my little boy. And I stayed clean for eight years after I got my perfect little boy. And I promised God I'd stay clean, but I got arrested on my son's twelfth birthday.

"My husband drank. We met when I was 12. We grew up in the same neighborhood and went to school together. I've known Bill my whole life, but we didn't start dating until I was 27. Then we got married.

"He got a DUI the day before we got married. On my wedding day, my dad bailed him out of jail.

"His dad drank and beat him and abused him both physically and mentally. He has overcome so much. He is a 100 times better father than his father ever was.

"But he drank every night – a case of beer every night. But, you know, he drank when we dated, so I don't know why I was surprised he drank after we married – for real. I thought he would change – I don't know why – but he didn't.

"We didn't have a sex life because you know what – you don't want to sleep with someone who's trashed. So, he'd tell me he was gonna' find somebody else, so I told him 'find somebody else.' And he did (laughs). He took up with somebody else.

"I didn't get married to get divorced. I remember walking down the aisle and my dad said 'You don't have to do this' and I was, like, all these people are here, you know. And I remember thinking, as I walked down the aisle, that I could get divorced. But then I remembered that once I promise God something, I work really hard at it.

"Sex didn't mean that much to me. It didn't matter to me because I had the perfect little boy.

"I stayed home for the first four years of our marriage, and we went without a lot of things. But I did things – like I was a nanny – anything that allowed me to take my son with me. Bill was really good about letting me stay home. The money didn't matter.

"Bill stopped drinking and I started using drugs when we separated. He took our lack of sex very personally. He was looking for companionship, and he took up with Patsy, a girl that we both know. I had gone to church with her my whole life.

"Our separation was terrible, terrible, terrible. I went to counseling and Bill wouldn't show up. I moved into my parents' home. I think I was 27 at that time.

"One day, after we separated, I went to our apartment to get some winter clothes and I found underwear on my kitchen table and roses and champagne. I phoned him about it, and he said, 'I don't know what you're talking about.'

"I said, 'are you telling me I'm not seeing what I'm seeing? I didn't know we were dating other people.' I was surprised but I was o.k. with it. I said, 'why didn't you just say you wanted a divorce?'

"Patsy's husband, Leon, came up to me in church and said, 'if you wouldn't have left Bill, I would still have a wife.' I said, 'we don't know how long they've been messing around.'

"One day I went to Bill and Patsy's house to pick up my son and Leon was there with a gun in his hand. It was terrible. I said, 'shoot whoever you want, but don't bring a gun around my child.' I picked up my little boy and ran.

"Leon ended up getting in a truck accident. He's paralyzed from the neck down. And Patsy went back to him. They still live together.

"One time Bill came to pick up our son at a birthday party. He was drunk when he walked in the door. I said, 'you know he can't leave with you' and one of our son's friends – he was eight or nine – said, 'your daddy's drunk.'

"Bill quit drinking after that and I'm still on drugs.

"I've been to two rehabs. In the last rehab they told me I have an emotional disorder. I feel other people's pain. The doctor wanted to put me on anti-depressants.

"There's a lot of pain here (jail). Sometimes I wake up in the middle of the night, and I can feel the pain of all these girls. Their men tell them they're gonna' come visit and then they don't. I've gotten to where I call it, in my mind, 'the Hope Line.' They're standing in the Hope Line, hopin' their man's going to come but he doesn't. Then it's terrible – the heartache that they feel. Sometimes I wake up in the middle of the night and I just cry because I know there's someone in here crying. I hate this place. (tears).

"I was happy as a child, but I cried a lot. It wasn't that I would cry for me. I'd cry for others. My dad used to say that I carry the guilt and suffering of the whole neighborhood – that nobody in the whole neighborhood needed to feel guilt or suffering because I would put it on my back and carry it.

"When I was pregnant, I cried every single day. Bill used to tell people 'All you have to say is 'two pats of butter' and she'll break down and cry.'

"Bill and I separated at the same time that our son was becoming independent and didn't need me much. That mattered a whole lot. That's when I started using drugs again.

"When I was 32 my car was hit by a drunk driver. I broke every bone in my face: my jaw, teeth, smashed my nose, everything. I had three different plastic surgeries. Then I started taking pain pills. That's what I'm here for – pain pills. When the doctor stopped prescribing them, I started buying them on the street.

"After the accident I started working in this bar. I was 38, almost 39. They were selling crystal meth out the back door of this bar. The police pulled over everyone leaving the bar. I got pulled over and I had Thorazine (prescribed for mood disorders), Vicodin and Percocet, all prescribed by a doctor for pain relief, but I didn't have them in the prescription bottles. Police said it's illegal to have those medicines on you if they're not in a prescription bottle. I was charged with three felonies. Ten days later, the same cop pulled me over and I had some crystal meth and more Vicodin – two more felonies. So I got five felonies in ten days.

"When I went in front of the judge, I was given five-years-probation. I went to my PO regularly for a whole year, but I wasn't honest with her. I'd quit using the pills for three days before seeing my PO so my urine drop would be clean.

"One day I took my son with me, and I was in a bathing suit. While at the PO's office, the police came and arrested me for the last two felonies. I didn't realize it, but the earlier five-years-probation was only for the first three felonies. Now I have to go to Judge Weisman's court to account for the first three felony charges and to Judge Kenrick's court for the other two. One wants to put me in Choices (the jail's drug rehab program) and the other wants to send me to prison in Vandalia.

"Right now, my bond is $210,000. Do I look like I'm worth a quarter of a million dollars? $210,000 for dropping dirty for drugs! Thankfully, while I was in jail, my boyfriend took the Thorazine, Vicodin and Percocet prescription bottles to the judge so he dismissed the first three felonies.

"After I got out of jail the last time, I just went crazy again. I started smoking crack, something I hadn't done in 11 years. I don't know why. I have sat and thought and thought and thought about my problems. I know there's a void in my life. I'm sure it's God.

"When I got out of jail the last time, I became a Sunday School teacher. I went to church three times weekly for five years. I enjoyed it.

"I spent all last June in rehab, got out, was clean for maybe six weeks. I started using again, dropped dirty again, went to rehab in December, spent Christmas in rehab away from my child.

It was really bad.

"I got out in January and went on house arrest. I was dropping clean, but only because I wasn't using from Friday to Monday. I had only two more days of house arrest left, and everything paid up. My PO said, 'we might cut you off early from house arrest' because I was doing so well. But I'm a functioning addict. I was smoking crack every day.

"I worked at Bob Evans. I'm a waitress. I made $108 a day – and I would pull extra shifts to support my drug use. At home I would shift my son into a different room with pizza and a video game, and I'd say 'you can't come in here.' I know he knew I was high a couple of times. He's a smart kid.

"I don't know what would help me stop using drugs. I'm scared to death that I'm going to get out and use again. I say I love my little boy but apparently, I love drugs more. (Cries). I don't know. I've been to so many NA and AA meetings.

"Psychiatrists say I have an emotional imbalance – that I need Prozac. I was evaluated twice: once at DART and once at Archway. Both told me about the emotional imbalance.

"I couldn't sleep when I got here. I'd cry all night. The day I got sentenced, they took me right from court to the psychiatrist. He put me on Prozac. I've been taking Prozac ever since then – and honestly, I have to tell you, I feel a more even keel. But my drug of choice is pills. I take drugs to cover up my feelings and make me feel better. Now, sometimes I want to cry, and I can't. I think they've got me on a real high dose of Prozac. But I almost feel like I'm doing the very same thing. I'm using Prozac now, instead of illegal drugs, to cover up my feelings...just substituting one drug for another.

"My parents still live in the same house they lived in when I was born. That's stability. My son does not know stability with me. I've moved three times in the last two years. I'm going to lose my apartment now because I'm here.

"My boyfriend brings my son to see me once a week. He came Saturday and brought his report card. His grades had dropped. He said, 'I don't want you to see it because you're going to be disappointed.' And I just cried because here I am in jail, and he thinks I'm going to be disappointed in him.

"I told him, 'I'm never disappointed in you. I'm disappointed _for_ you because I know you can do better."

* * * * *

In court, Melissa was sentenced to five months in jail and required to enroll in Choices, a 120- day, in-house drug rehab program which will be followed by outpatient meetings. Presumably she continued taking the prescribed Prozac because her "emotional imbalance" stabilized.

Following her release from jail and Choices, she was never again arrested. At the time of this writing, she is 55 years-old and her son is in his 30's.

The United States incarcerates a higher percentage of our citizens than any other country, including Russia and China. What a blessing it would be if, instead of short-sighted, million-dollar incarceration "fixes," we in the U.S. would offer justice-involved-women the opportunity to spend a period of time (three months, six months, etc.) in therapeutic facilities where teams of health workers could assess their physical, social and emotional health needs and offer long-term solutions.

CHAPTER EIGHT:
SHELANA: DRUG DEALER

WHO IS MY FATHER? WHERE IS MY MOTHER?

Shelana was 46 years old when I met her in the Buzz Westfall Justice Center in Clayton MO.

She wrote her life story in 3 ½ pages. Because she preferred talking over writing, she gave me much additional information about herself in the several private conversations we had after she submitted her written words. I have incorporated this verbal information into her story.

IN SHELANA'S WORDS

"I'm not sure how or where to begin my story. I have come a long way and I thank God for the distance I've travelled. I am now retired and disabled at the age of 46. I have had several different careers: ambulance driver, bartender, prostitute, paralegal, factory worker, office worker and truck driver. I recently sold my 18-wheeler because I fell from the truck, hurt myself and can no longer drive.

"My mother disappeared in 1960 shortly after my brother, Rennie, was born. I was one at that time and had no memories of her. Our mother left Rennie and me with Henry's parents, Henry being the man I thought was my father. Henry had married another woman – Janie – and moved out-of-state so, although I knew his name, I did not know him. Rennie and I lived with our grandmother.

"When I was 11, our grandmother died. Henry returned for his mother's funeral where I met him for the first time. Without our grandmother, we had no home, so Henry took me and Rennie to Los Angeles to live with him and Janie. Janie was very good to me.

"From the time I was 12 until I was 15, Henry raped me. I hated him. This made me think that sex was love and it took me a long time to realize that this was not the case. I should have told Janie, but I didn't want to hurt her, but also because I thought it was my fault. It was really hard, at age 12, to meet the man I thought was my father and have him do this to me.

"I dropped out of school and ran away, when I was a sophomore, to get away from Henry. I prostituted for survival money. I also started drinking alcohol and smoking marijuana.

"The law caught me, returned me to Henry and placed me on probation. My probation officer needed my mother's name, and I overheard Henry say Laura Gellerfahl. My search for her began. I spent every spare minute in the library going through city phone directories. I wrote a letter to every Gellerfahl I found.

"My search took five years but, when I was 18, I received a letter from my mother's brother. He gave me a phone number for my mother. I called her for the first time in December, 1977. She thought I had died in a car accident and was shocked to learn that I was alive.

"In January 1978, she flew into California where I met her for the first time. We were in the newspaper and on TV: 'Daughter finds mother after 18 years.' Laura took me to Florida to live with her.

"Shortly after we got there, I found out I was pregnant, and she took me to have an abortion. I felt bad about that for many years. But, even feeling so bad about this, it wasn't my first abortion. The first was a boy. I was 16 years old and five months pregnant when I aborted him.

"While I lived with Laura, I learned that she had been married 13 times, had a total (including Rennie and me) of eight children by eight different men. In addition, she had adopted two of her grandchildren. While with her I met her other children.

"Laura also told me that Henry was Rennie's birth father, but not mine. She introduced me to my real birth father and his wife, and I learned that I have three half-brothers through them. We don't stay in touch, but I hear from my birth father every Christmas.

"Laura's husband helped me get my GED, and I began classes in a community college. Eventually I earned an Associate Degree with a 3.8 grade point average (GPA).

"I have been married four times. My first marriage lasted six months. We used a lot of drugs: pot, acid, cocaine. We had a $300/day habit.

"I married my second husband the day I left the first one. This second husband is the father of my daughter born in 1981, and my son born in '82. I had post-partum depression after my son was born and I attempted suicide on aspirin and Tylenol.

"My drug use increased, and the Department of Family Services (DFS) gave my children to their father. He took them out of state. I didn't know, for a long time, where they were.

"In 1986 I was kidnapped, tied up, taken to the desert and beaten. The responsible person was a girl who had dated the guy I was currently dating.

"In 1989 I stopped using drugs and remained drug free for several years.

"When my son was 12 (1994) his father phoned and told me that our son's behavior was out of control. He returned my son to me. My son is now in prison for stealing a car. He was diagnosed as having bi-polar and obsessive-compulsive disorders, just like me. That same year my daughter refused to see me – said she didn't want to have anything to do with me.

"In 1998 police arrested me at my job in Missouri and charged me with kidnapping, attempted murder, sexual assault and five other felony accounts.

They shackled me and flew me to California where I was supposed to have committed these crimes. They released me when authorities learned that I had not been in California during that time, and that I had not committed those crimes. The person who accused me was the same girl who had kidnapped and beaten me 12 years earlier.

"In that same year (1998) I was diagnosed with hepatitis and placed on interferon. The medicine kept me awake for several days and I got depressed. I went back to stay with my mother and rested. While there my mother was diagnosed with cancer, and I was able to take care of her.

"Things piled up on me in 1999. My third husband whom I married in 1989 was a heavy drug user and died of a heroin overdose. That same year (1999) my mother died of cancer, I turned 40, and I became a grandmother. It was too much stress at one time, and I started drinking a lot. That led to me using drugs again.

"In 2000 I married my fourth husband. He does not drink or use drugs and doesn't want me to do it either. I did stop drinking but I continued to use drugs. I started dealing drugs too –BIG TIME.

"Every two to three weeks I drove to California, picked up 10 pounds of methamphetamines, paid $10,000 per pound for it, and drove it back to Missouri. I kept what I needed for my addiction and sold the rest for $16,000 per pound. Police arrested me twice in one week for dealing drugs. They wanted to give me eight years in prison but, instead, put me into drug rehab. Once I completed the program, they released me on seven years parole.

In 2004 I got depressed again. I had been diagnosed – like my son – with bi-polar and obsessive-compulsive-disorder. I took a bunch of pills, trying to kill myself. A medical staff had to pump my stomach.

"Today (2006) I don't feel suicidal, but I'm worried about the amount of time I'll be confined to the federal prison in Texas (for transporting meth across state lines). My husband plans to drive our motor home there, so he'll be able to visit me often. But if my sentence is several years, I wonder if he'll stay faithful".

* * * * *

A few years after police transported Shelana to the federal prison in Texas, I was in Texas for a conference. I stopped at the facility hoping to visit Shelana and another of my former students who were imprisoned there. However, because I had not made previous arrangements for the visit, officers were unable to give me visiting privileges. I did write both women to let them know I had made the attempt. I received return notes thanking me and telling me that they were doing well. I have had no other contact with, or news about, Shelana.

Shefali Tsabary, PhD writes, in *The Conscious Parent*, that children need two things from their parents: affirmation of their being and loving support to contain their actions.

> (Shefali Tsabary, PhD, *The Conscious Parent: Transforming ourselves, Empowering our Children*. Vancouver, Canada: Namaste Publishing. 2010.)

Shelana's story makes it clear what can happen to a child who lacks those two supportive pillars.

I suspect that, in general, society judges drug dealers more harshly than it judges drug users. However, I wonder if dealers, like Shelana, would become dealers if they had had healthy parental love and guidance during their childhood/teen years. I try to imagine the emotional pain held in Shelana's heart as a result of not even knowing her mother's name; experiencing, at age 11, the death of her grandmother; being incested for three years by the man she thought was her father; dropping out of school and running away from the incest; prostituting for survival money; finding herself alone, addicted, pregnant, and having an abortion – all before the age of 18 when she found her birth mother.

There is no doubt that drug dealers menace our society. However, so long as our societal focus remains on the dealing instead of providing therapy to heal the childhood/teenaged traumas that birth the drug dealing, the menace will remain.

CHAPTER NINE:
WOMEN WITH MENTAL DISORDERS

... many offenders have a variety of ... neurodevelopmental, neurocognitive and intellectual deficits and disorders that are fundamentally linked to their criminality...

(William R. Kelly, Robert Pitman & William Streusand. From *Retribution to Public Safety: Disruptive Innovation of American Criminal Justice*. Rowman & Littlefield Publishing Co., 2017, p. 6).

*T*he next two stories will be about women with mental disorders. First, a bit of information about mental disorders.

People with unusual behaviors tend to scare us. We don't understand why "they" aren't like "us." We may feel embarrassed by them if they're members of our family. We may want to help them, but lack the knowledge, funds or power to do so.

Since 1952 psychiatrists have classified mental disorders in a book known as the *Diagnostic and Statistical Manual* (DSM).

The DSM has been revised and updated five times since 1952. The current one, DSM-5, published in 2013, lists more than 300 mental disorders. They are categorized under the headings of Adjustment, Anxiety, Eating, Personality, Mood, Psychotic, Sleep Dissociation, Sexual and Impulse Control Disorders, and others.

People with mental disorders need medical/psychological help. However, when they break laws, police tend to jail them instead of transporting them to behavioral health institutions.

Most of the women whose stories are told in this book have some form of mental disorder. However, I used their stories to illustrate – not those disorders – but the traumas they experienced during their formative years – traumas which were the reasons for, or contributed to, their entrance into the drug world and/or prostitution, and crime.

In the two chapters which follow this one, you will read snippets of the stories of women who were jailed because of behaviors related to their mental disorders. But you will not read about the incidents in their early life which may have contributed to those mental disorders. I do not have that information.

Instead, you will find information gleaned from their class work, their behavior in classes, and my interactions with them.

In my 26 years working with these women, I have had women with diagnoses of obsessive- compulsive disorder (OCD), bi-polar disorder, anxiety disorder, skin picking and cutting disorder, traumatic brain injury (TBI), simple depression, feeding disorders and others. Many of them have dual diagnoses (a psychiatric disorder together with a drug use disorder). Large numbers of them (over and above those who have accidentally overdosed on illegal drugs) have attempted suicide, some of them multiple times.

In the two chapters which follow you will read about Ce'janna who was always in trouble with the law, and Beatrice whose diagnosis was paranoid schizophrenia.

CHAPTER TEN:
CE'JANNA

SCHIZOPHRENIA AND BI-POLAR DISORDER

Ce'janna, aged about 50, spoke rapidly, excitedly and often. She possessed an excellent vocabulary, but moved rapidly from one topic to another, one phrase or sentence seemingly unrelated to that which preceded it. At times I found it difficult, even impossible, to follow her ideas. Although I felt rude when doing it, I learned to interrupt her in mid-sentence and re-introduce the topic which she had originally been addressing. She never took offense with my interruptions but, in a short time, moved back into her flight of ideas.

Ce'janna had experienced many run-ins with police. "They know me well," she said. "I don't let them get away with anything."

Previously, police had arrested her for what she called her neighborhood ministry. "I create summer jobs for teens and help the kids set up checking accounts. They need to know how to use the bank. I created a playground for the younger children and police arrested me for that."

I never had total clarity about how these activities constituted crimes but, if I understood Ce'janna correctly, police cited her for operating businesses without a license (creating summer jobs, collecting the money for the teens and pre-teens and helping the youth bank it), and either trespassing or confiscating unused public property for the playground. Because she saw no reason why she should not help the youth, she threatened to sue law enforcement.

Ce'janna's most recent tangle with police followed a theft in her home. Police made a record of her losses. However, "they didn't report that my closet was empty. The thief stole all of my clothes."

Because the police report lacked this information, the insurance company would not compensate her for the loss. What followed was a scuffle with police that resulted in Ce'janna's arrest.

I asked Ce'janna's about her diagnoses. She said she has bi-polar disorder (previously known as manic-depression), and schizophrenia for which she refuses to take prescribed drugs. "I'm not going to let them get me on drugs."

She hears voices that tell her things to do. "I can tell which voices are good and which are evil," she said. "I do what the good voices tell me and ignore the bad ones."

"What does your doctor say about that?" I asked.

"I don't tell him, she said. "It's none of his business."

It is likely that Ce'janna's skirmishes with police will continue and possibly increase in severity unless, with therapy, she grows willing to take her prescribed medications. Or, unless police become educated to the mental health needs of people like Ce'janna.

Some cities, like Nashville TN, divert people with mental disorders to mental health courts instead of jailing them. The mental health courts include a system of employees who have backgrounds in human services, social sciences, and humanities. It is headed by a Judge.

Other cities and counties have post-arrest mental health courts to which people with mental health disorders can be diverted post-arrest. However, case workers in jails have little time to identify and divert arrestees who have mental health problems. Unless that situation changes, our jails will continue to be filled with people who have mental health issues.

CHAPTER ELEVEN: BEATRICE

PARANOID SCHIZOPHRENIA

*B*eatrice, a woman in her mid-forties, seldom spoke in class. However, her written work showed an extensive vocabulary, depth of insight and an analytical mind. I felt impressed with her intelligence and with her written responses to homework questions.

One day after class, she asked to speak privately with me. Our conversation went something like this.

"I need you to help me. My son and my lawyer say that I'm mentally ill and I'm not."

I felt confused. I, a registered nurse, had not observed any signs of mental illness in her.

"I don't understand," I said. "Why do they say that?"

"I overheard several conversations between my husband, Paul, and his lawyer. They wanted to kill me, so I killed Paul first. I couldn't convince the jury that it was self-defense, so the judge sentenced me to life in prison.

"Prison was terrible. Paul's lawyer worked with the prison staff and encouraged them to kill me.

They poisoned food, and I didn't know which food it was, so I didn't accept food from any container unless the woman in front of me in line took some first. In the dayroom I had to sit with my back to the wall to make sure no one attacked me from behind. Sometimes I could smell stuff leaking from the pipes in my cell. They tried to gas me."

"My children don't believe me. They say I'm paranoid. They hired a lawyer to reopen my case. They want a judge to put me in a mental hospital. But I'm not paranoid. It really happened."

I asked if she realized how impossible it would be for a lawyer to involve an entire prison staff in such a conspiracy, without at least one person blowing the whistle on the plan.

She responded that she knew it sounded incredible but that it really happened.

We talked for a while after that but, in the end, I told her I was sorry I couldn't help her, but that I wished her well. She thanked me for listening to her dilemma.

In her retrial, the judge found Beatrice "not guilty (of killing her husband) by reason of insanity." He sentenced her to life in prison for people with mental disorders.

I have had no further contact with Beatrice. However, given the fact that new anti-psychotic drugs are now available, I wonder if they are being prescribed for her in the prison hospital and, if so, whether her psychotic thought processes disappeared. I hope that the prison medical officers have educated themselves about new anti-psychotic drugs and prescribed them for her. I also hope that, if that has happened, Beatrice has been offered therapy to work through the grief and guilt she must feel for having killed her husband.

CHAPTER TWELVE:
WOMEN WITH
INTELLECTUAL DISABILITIES

An intellectual disability is "a disability characterized by significant limitations both in intellectual functioning (reasoning, learning, problem solving) and in adaptive behavior, which covers a range of everyday social and practical skills. This disability originates before the age of 18.

(American Association of Intellectual and Developmental Disabilities quoted in Stephanie O. Hubach. *Same lake different BOAT: Coming Alongside People Touched by Disability.* P&R Publishing: Phillipsburg, New Jersey. Revised and Updated. 2020.)

*A*t least one and sometimes two women with intellectual deficiencies – often called mental challenges – enroll in my monthly course in the jail. They come with a variety of impediments. For example, Jill and Paula could read but had little understanding of those words.

Sometime Anna comprehended what she read and sometimes she did not. She had great difficulty with spelling and sentence composition. The jail does not allow staples or paper clips in the classroom, so I give each woman daily sets of 15-20 untethered pages. Although those pages are numbered, Anna had trouble remembering that page five follows page four or that page eight precedes page nine.

Women seated on either side of her tried to help, but she never caught on. That part of her brain refused to function.

The Arc of the US is an organization founded in 1950 by parents of people with intellectual and developmental disabilities. Its national center is located in Washington DC. to promote and protect the human rights of people with intellectual and developmental disabilities.

To paraphrase the Arc's literature: it is true that people with intellectual disabilities do sometimes commit crimes, even serious crimes. Sometimes, too, they admit to crimes which they did not commit. Reasons for this are varied, including but not limited to:

- A desire to hide their disability,
- Feeling overwhelmed by police presence,
- Not understanding the instructions or commands,
- Saying things they believe the police want to hear,
- Difficulties with describing details or facts of an offense,

[They also may]:

- Be easily influenced,
- Believe the perpetrator is their "friend,"
- Be unaware of the seriousness or danger of a situation.

The chapters which follow tell, in fuller detail, the stories of three women with intellectual disabilities, whom I met in jail.

CHAPTER THIRTEEN:
SHARON

DEVELOPMENTALLY CHALLENGED OR MISDIAGNOSED?

*S*haron a petite, quiet woman appeared to be in her mid-thirties. Her class papers showed low average intelligence. She wrote in simple statements and had difficulty spelling. For example, she wrote trajic for tragic; papper for paper. She capitalized many words unnecessarily as, for example, Mom and dad Split up; turned over To The State, etc.

In the story that follows, I have made corrections to these misspellings. Given her traumas and that she dropped out of school in grade five, she is to be commended that her written words are decipherable.

IN SHARON'S WORDS

"My name is Sharon. Oldest daughter to Milton and Sally. I have a 24-year-old little sister, Kim, who's a 'Hooter's Girl' model. I also had a sister, Carrie Ann, who died in 1974. She was two and I was five. We were playing in a boat. I got out and left my little sister in it. When she tried to get out, she fell and cracked her head against a rock and died.

"It was tragic for the family. I, myself, do remember it clearly as if it happened yesterday. I carried the blame for years, until about four years ago when I was in rehab and started dealing with it. Mom and dad split up three years later when I was eight.

"I quit school early in the fifth grade. I'm not very smart and I couldn't control my behavior. The principal hit me with a ruler for talking too much. I grabbed the ruler and whacked her back. We both ended up with bleeding hands. For a while I went to a group home for children with behavior problems, but I got into a fight with the principal and broke his nose.

"My drinking started when I was nine or ten. I smoked cigarettes at nine too and I inhaled at 10.

"Dad married Jackie when I was 11. Jackie and I did not get along. I had anger issues and I used to beat on her and not listen. Mom married Gene when I was 12. At that same age, I was raped by my 19-year-old cousin. Then I began drugs (marijuana, cocaine, and meth). My family turned me over to the custody of the state and I was put into a variety of group homes.

"When I was 14, I ran away from one of those homes and was gang raped by a bunch of guys – seemed like 15 or 16 of them. They shoved me into a basement and were going to put me in a dumpster but, in the end, they didn't.

"I got married when I was 16, and I am a proud mother of five: 16, 14, 12, 5 ½ and 2 ½ years, although, because I was in prison, I missed out on raising the three oldest. And, if I keep on, I'm going to miss out on the two little ones.

"I was diagnosed, at age 18 or 20, with bipolar disorder. Later, they added Schizophrenic (my translation of Sharon's spelling "Phcitydric") Tendencies because I can't sit still. I rock a lot. I have had visual hallucinations since I was a child. I didn't tell anybody about the hallucinations because I thought they made me special. I also 'fly off the handle' and isolate when I'm not on medication.

"My children's father left me this past October, and I lost my grandmother that month too. My grandmother and I were very, very close and she raised by second oldest child for me. They lived in Arizona the past five years. I had talked to my PO about moving there to take care of her when I got out of Bridgeway (drug rehab). She (the PO) had started the paperwork.

Grandma died the day after my birthday before I got out of treatment. She was neglected by the people at the home she had to be placed in, until I could get out there.

"Because of using drugs, I have lost our trailer and everything. I feel as though I'm weak. When I was 23 or 24, I attempted suicide using pills and alcohol. I was home alone. My husband told me that, when he came home, he thought I was drunk and passed out on the bed. He said my daughter, 4 ½ at the time, got up on the bed and patted my face, trying to wake me up. When that didn't work, she started hitting me. My husband saw it was more than drunkenness and got me to the hospital.

"After that I promised I would not attempt suicide again. However, I still have thoughts of suicide, and think my family would be better off if I were dead. After my suicide attempt, I had electric shock treatments for depression.

"My original case was for stealing from my mother and stepdad. They were on vacation at the time. I thought I took rolls of quarters, about $300 worth. I left them an IOU to be paid when I got my check. The money turned out to be old, rare silver coins that had been in my stepdad's family for years.

"Police arrested me for drug possession several times. Once I did 120 days of drug rehab in the Vandalia Prison. I stayed clean a year and five months after that, so I know I can do it.

"In another case I was charged with burglary of a family I didn't know. It turned out that police were searching the house for meth. Police arrested me for driving with stolen merchandise in the car. I was sentenced to drug rehab at Bridgeway, but I got kicked out of treatment and went on the run for a while. Then I turned myself in.

"My self-esteem has always been very low, but now it's getting better. And I always seem to think I need a man to depend on, but I now know that's not true.

The drugs I use are pot and meth. I used heroin for a little while, but I've been clean from that for three years.

"Three years ago, I was diagnosed with Hepatitis C. My family is pretty much done with me.

"I'm doing a lot of work now with the grief guilt I've carried for all these years, and I know I don't need drugs anymore to cover up the pain".

* * * * *

Trauma has a deeper and more far-reaching impact than everyday stress. Women who've experienced traumatic events describe feelings of intense fear, shame, helplessness, anger, and horror. These are normal reactions to abnormal or extreme situations.

(Stephanie Covington. *A Healing Journey: A Workbook for Women*. Center City MN: Hazelton Publishing. Second Edition, 2016).

When I talked to Sharon and read her story, it seemed obvious that she was traumatized by guilt. I suspect that guilt also plays a part in her psychiatric diagnoses.

However, because her story illustrates the relationship of trauma to behavioral and mental disabilities, I decided to insert her story into this section.

It is not hard to imagine the distress the five-year-old, Sharon, experienced as her two-year-old sister exited the boat, hit her head on a rock and died. Pandemonium must have followed: screaming, crying; scores of neighbors converging on the home in response to the wailing; police, fire and ambulance sirens; medics trying to revive the child; police asking questions.

What must all of this have done to the psyche of the five-year-old child, who was just learning to read? No wonder she began drinking and smoking cigarettes at age nine or ten! No wonder she became disruptive and dropped out of school!

The tragic death of Sharon's sister was followed by the breakup in the parental marriage and, within two years, the introduction of stepparents into the family circle. Sharon's life unraveled, like a ball of yarn, until she ended up sentenced to seven years in prison. While there, I hope she received grief therapy to heal her pain and free her from guilt.

In 2018, the United States Congress passed the *Federal Prison Reform and Redemption Act (First Step Act).*

Part of the Act requires a detailed interview with each prisoner. The goal is to determine the individual's risk level for parole. Part of the interview focuses on traumas which the woman has sustained during her life. The information gathered will provide opportunities for the healing of the traumas uncovered during the interviews.

Unfortunately, this act applies only to citizens in the Federal Justice System. My hope is that, in time, it will apply to women in the State Prison System too.

We, as a society, do ourselves no favor when we fail to provide trauma care for at-risk children and teens. Any time a child, like Sharon, acts out in school, a bell should ring in the teacher's ears saying, "this child needs help!" and resources should be available for those children, even if the parents cannot afford it.

Both in general society and in jail, I have witnessed adults who believed they were intellectually disabled. Yet with individual attention, help in healing their traumas and identifying their strengths, they have earned their G.E.D.'s and begun college. I believe Sharon has that potential.

Since the 2012 Sandy Hook School shootings in Newton CT, schools have brought counselors on board to deal with children's traumas. That is a very positive sign that we have begun to care for the children. It also opens the possibility that we, as a society, will soon realize that mental health care is far less expensive than the costs of incarceration.

CHAPTER FOURTEEN: ALICIA

DEVELOPMENTALLY CHALLENGED

*A*licia, a beautiful 19-year-old woman with long silky blonde hair, exuded the delight of a four-year-old opening birthday gifts. Her youthful energy contrasted sharply with the sedateness of the other women, aged 25 to 43, seated with her in the jail classroom. Each time I posed a question to the group, Alicia waved her hand saying, "I know. I know."

When I called on her, she responded with something totally unrelated to the topic. "I like puppies. Do you have any puppies?"

The older women mothered the child that Alicia was. "You did good," they'd say or "You are such a fine young lady. I am so proud of you."

After class one day, Lt. Perry, head (CO) – ordinarily called a "white shirt" to distinguish his higher role from that of most officers who wore blue and were called "blue shirts," - asked me, "Can you do anything for Alicia? You can see that this is no place for her."

"Why was she arrested?" I asked. "What brought her here?"

Lt Perry explained that a group of teenaged boys in her neighborhood taught her to hotwire cars. "When she gets into the cars to drive, the boys run off laughing and she gets arrested. The teens think it's funny. 'Alicia thinks they like her. This is her third arrest. Her mother has given up on her and won't let her go home."

I phoned Options for Justice, a St. Louis Organization which guides developmentally challenged adults through the Justice System. Options enlisted help from the Center for Women in Transition (CWIT), an organization which assesses the needs of women exiting the CJS, and provides gender-based, trauma-informed case management services for them.

However, both Options for Justice and CWIT are not-for-profit (NFP) organizations. They do not exist in most cities and do not have the resources to provide for every incarcerated person with developmental challenges.

Title II of the *Adults with Disabilities Act* (ADA) requires jails and prisons to provide needed services and activities for inmates with disabilities. But costs related to the burgeoning jail and prison populations leave little money for these services.

For example, the 1200 inmate Buzz Westfall Justice Center where I volunteered, had one caseworker (CW) for each 250 men and women housed there. Each CW is charged with impossible responsibilities:

- make an intake assessment, and interview each inmate before her release to home or transfer to prison,
- research and update records,
- coordinate health needs,
- contact county agencies (for example the Department of Family Services for women with children in foster care),
- liaison with the public defender's office,
- attend meetings, etc.

Given a 40-hour work week, a CW has time to spend less than 10 minutes per week with each arrestee in her charge). Clearly, the CW's have little time to attend to the special needs of women like Alicia. This is probably the reason that Lt. Perry asked me, instead of the CW, to help Alicia.

Alicia's academic abilities are very limited. She can neither read, write nor comprehend simple math. She is unable to plan for tomorrow or to prioritize her needs for today. She is very comfortable socially but cannot distinguish between people who can help her and those who would use her. She can attend to her own cleanliness needs but other than that, can function only within her family home or in a sheltered workshop.

Once Alicia was released from the jail, the Center for Women in Transition conferred with her mother who had a change of heart and allowed her to return home.

CHAPTER FIFTEEN: DAHLIA

INTELLECTUALLY CHALLENGED:

USED AND ABUSED

Dahlia, a tall thin woman weighing less than 90 pounds, had minimal writing skills, so I taped her life story which she shared verbally with me. Her worn, leathered face and missing bottom teeth spoke of poverty, and aged her beyond her 50 years.

In class, she humbly accepted help with her reading, and thanked classmates who prompted her when she paused before unrecognized words.

IN DAHLIA'S WORDS

"My daddy entered the military when I was young – maybe one or two years old. I don't remember him. While he was away, my mama got pregnant. My parents divorced and each remarried. I have an older brother, three half-brothers and a half-sister.

"I like to work. I've held lots of jobs: nurse aide, carpet roller, UPS factory worker, Salvation Army worker, cook in a nursing home, clerk in a welfare office.

"I had a wonderful childhood. Mama was a schoolteacher and Donnie, my stepfather, was a musician. We travelled every summer: New Orleans, Chicago, New York, all over the country. Sometimes we went to Mississippi to visit my mama's mama.

"Donnie walked me to school every day. He took me places and showed lots of love. He never whipped me. He sat me down and talked to me like a parent should. We did everything like a good family – went to church on Sunday and sat down for dinner together every night. It was good times.

"When I was twelve, I came home from school and the police were all there at the house, and I didn't know drugs was in the house. It was the FBI. Donnie was selling drugs and mama was using heroin. Then the police took us kids over to Donnie's mother, Gramma Roamer's house.

"They let my mama go the next day, but not Donnie. I kept on wondering 'where was Donnie at?' Mama wouldn't tell me. She'd say he was out of town. He was travelling. She got a letter from him saying for me to put a candle in the window every time I'd be lonely for him. And I put the candle in the window every night. And I would see, like a vision, that he was there with me. I would pray that he would come home.

"He stayed in prison 37 years, and just got out two years ago. I went to his house, after he got out of prison, and I smelled something bad. I looked in the mailbox, and in the window, and I seen it was empty up in the house.

"The last time I talked to him was June 21st and he died July 27th of this year. I went over to Gramma Roamer's house. They cremated him and Gramma Roamer's got his ashes, and she gave me the obituary, and I told her I don't want it because I don't want to believe he's gone away again.

Mama died of breast cancer while Donnie was still in prison. When he came home, Gramma Roamer said Donnie told her that he stood there at mama's grave in the cemetery, and it just took the life away from him and he didn't have no business to live no more. So, he died of a massive heart attack.

"When I was 21, my mama was on heroin so bad that she sold me to the drug man to get her drugs and he raped me. Mama had sent me down there to his house, and I didn't know what I was going down there for. He gave me an envelope and told me to go to the other room. I went in the back room and then he told me 'take your clothes off.'

"I said, 'take my clothes off? What for?' Then he had a gun, so I took my clothes off.

"When I got back to the house, I poured the dope in the toilet stool, and I called my mama all kinds of names. I told her she was dirty, and I hated her, and I wished she was dead. And, really, last year is when I forgave her. She died several years ago, but I wrote a letter to her anyway and then tore it up. I told her that I couldn't keep on holding this hate inside me.

"With the rape and all, it seemed like it was a flashback coming back on me, and I went to drug treatment. I was hearing voices and having mood swings.

"I been clean five years now. I had asthma too and was going through menopause, so I saw a psychiatrist and he gave me medicine. I'm still taking Benadryl, Nexium and Prozac.

"I started drugs when I was 30 because of flashbacks. I used crack cocaine from age 30-44. I thought it would ease my problems. I couldn't believe my mama did that to me. I was her only girl. I'd work and make money and just blow it. But, like I said, I've been clean for five years now.

"I went to school to the 11th grade. I got pregnant at the age of 15. He was my first sweetheart. Me and my daughter grew up together. She lives down south now and has her own baby.

"Once, after I put her dope in the toilet, mama called me an unfit mother. She put me out of the house and took my baby away from me. But I got a job and a place to stay and took my baby back.

"I was a cook in a nursing home when I was arrested. The home was owned by a lady who opened her own company. [I was arrested because] she said I was stealing her check book and writing checks to myself, and then taking them to the bank and cashing them. But I wasn't. What I found out later is that she was in money trouble. The checks she paid me bounced and that's when she called police and told them I forged them checks.

"I gave my receipts to my lawyer (a public defender) and everything, but it didn't count for nothin'. They gave me four days in jail and five-years-probation. My lawyer said if I didn't plead guilty, I could get 15 years in prison. So I pleaded guilty even though I weren't. I had to pay the bank $1,000 and I had to pay $700 to the nursing home bank. So, I worked for nothin'.

"My daughter called me to come to Georgia (while I was on probation in St. Louis), because she got hurt. A bullet hit her chest when she was coming home from work – missed her heart by one inch. I moved there to help her, but I got in trouble driving on an expired license. I served five months in a Georgia Jail for that.

"Then the jail there called St. Louis because I didn't get the o.k. from my probation officer to leave Missouri. (People on probation or parole need their probation officer's permission to move from one address to another, or to leave the state. Failure to do that is considered a 'technical violation' of the terms of probation. As such probationers can be returned to jail or prison.)

"So I came home and turned myself in, and I'm doing 60 days (in jail) now. When I get out, I won't be on no more papers (probation). I'll go to my daughter's place for a while to get my affairs straightened out there, and then I'll come back to be with my husband and baby.

"I'm scared now, though, 'cause my husband's daddy told him he shouldn't be married to no negro lady."

* * * * *

Based on Dahlia's love of working and the variety of jobs with which she has supported herself, she certainly has an average amount of practical intelligence. However, she lacks the assertiveness to question authority figures and, therefore, cannot promote her own self-interests and improve her possibilities.

In the past 40 years, common law practice has allowed prosecuting attorneys to present either/or offers (plea deals) to defendants: plead guilty or face a huge number of years in prison. This strikes fear in the hearts of defendants, particularly those with dependent children and those with limited mental capacities. They plead guilty even though they know they are not.

> Some innocent defendants will rationally forgo their right to trial and plead guilty. A portion of them may be risk-averse or want to get on with their lives as soon as possible. Others are wooed into pleading guilty by the plain truth that prosecutors offer the best pleas in the weakest cases. And the weakest cases, of course, are those with the highest chance of implicating an innocent defendant.
>
> (Daniel Medwed PhD. *Prosecution Complex: America's Race To Convict and Its Impact on the Innocent*. New York University Press, 2012).

Why do prosecuting attorneys promote plea deals? One reason is that plea deals take less time than court trials. Another important reason is that, in many states, the prosecuting attorney is an elected office. To increase his or her chances of re-election, prosecuting attorneys want to be identified as "tough on crime." The more people they put into prison, the higher their chances of being re-elected.

Another problem for Dahlia was poverty and an overworked public defender. A person with adequate finances would hire a private attorney who, exercising due diligence, would question Dahlia's intellectual ability to plan the action for which she was charged in the nursing home. Dahlia would, then, have been acquitted, presuming as seems to be the case, that she was not guilty of that charge. Had she been acquitted on that nursing home legal charge, she would not have been on probation when she fled to Georgia to care for her daughter. Thus, she would not have received the technical violation which placed her in jail this last time.

Records show that police frequently "pull over" men and women of color for "driving while black," a practice known as "profiling." To illustrate, a minister in St. Louis told me that police stopped him and a friend one night as they left a restaurant. After ordering the two men out of the car and checking the minister's driver's license, the officer told them they could go. When the minister asked why he had been stopped, the officer replied that he presumed the car was stolen because it was a Cadillac, the presumption being, of course, that a man of color could not own an expensive car.

Dahlia is no longer incarcerated. She was charged, in a later year, with a misdemeanor. She paid a fine and was released. She has had no further record of arrests in Missouri. I have lost contact with her, but I hope she is enjoying life with her husband and son in Missouri or with her son, daughter and granddaughter in Georgia.

CHAPTER SIXTEEN: INCEST

*I*n the next two chapters you will read stories about two incest victims: Leisha who suffered from body dysmorphia and Mattie who was socialized, through play, into incest. Before we meet them, however, an introduction to incest is in order.

Incest is a sexual encounter initiated by a family member or by an extended family member that damages the child. By 'extended family' we mean an aunt, uncle, in-law, stepparent, cousin, friend of the family, teacher, coach, another child, clergy, or anyone that has betrayed the child's trust.

In the United States, incest of young women by men in positions of power (employers and potential employers) receives a lot of attention (#MeToo). It is called "rape" but is actually incest because it is perpetrated by men who have ongoing power relationships with the women.

The problem exists far beyond the workplace: in churches, sports, the political arena, schools and family homes. Because it is well hidden within contemporary society, incest receives minimal attention from the press.

Only in late 2021 did the U.S. begin to listen to the cries of young women athletes who, over a period of years, reported incest by their tennis physician.

In past years, five or six of every eight women in the course I taught in jail reported incest in their background. As the years passed, the number increased to seven out of eight women. Additionally, I want to note that each of these women was surprised to learn that she was not the only one in the course who had been incested. Learning that she is not alone is an eye-opener for the women, as well as a bit of a relief. It breaks through the silence barrier surrounding incest. It also removes, from each woman, the false belief that the incest was her fault.

Most of the women who, in the course I taught, reported childhood incest also wrote, "I don't trust anyone." This is a sad situation. It means that the incest victim lives in a state of insecurity, unable to rely on the words and actions of others.

The women reported that their mothers' boyfriends were the most frequent incest perpetrators, but birth fathers, stepfathers, grandfathers, step-grandfathers, brothers, step-brothers, uncles, cousins, neighbors and even mothers were implicated. Very few women, said the trauma occurred one to three times. For the majority, it occurred several times weekly for multiple years.

According to Dr. Peter A. Levine, trauma releases our innate fight, flight response. Adrenalin is released into the victim's body. The adrenalin energy enables her to protect herself (fight) or run away (flight).

> (Peter A. Levine with Ann Frederick. *Waking the Tiger: Healing Trauma.* Berkeley, CA: North Atlantic Books, 1997).

However, a child in an incest situation with a normal sized adult or teen, has neither the physical ability to fight nor to flee – so she cannot release the energy. Being unable to either fight or flee, she freezes with the energy trapped inside of her.

> Once the threat level is perceived as inescapable…we progress to…*a profound stage of hopelessness and helplessness.* (Italics mine.) Our bodies and spirit collapse while our metabolic processes (including digestion, respiration, circulation, and energy production) shut down… In this state, with both the accelerator and brake fully engaged…[we] are left in the sheer hell realm of trauma, paralyzed with terror, while experiencing eruptions of blind rage yet devoid of the sustained energy to act.

(Peter A. Levine, PhD. *Trauma and Memory: Brain and Body in a Search for the Living Past*. Berkeley CA: North American Books, 2015. 45-46).

I suspect that this profound state of hopelessness and helplessness is responsible for these children and youth's vulnerability to rape throughout their lives.

Children want and expect affection (love, cuddling and hugging) from family members, especially those in parenting positions. Instead, the parental figure's incestual act confuses the child who also suffers physical, emotional and sexual pain.

Natalia, repeatedly incested in childhood, told me she suffers flashbacks and nightmares: "It's dark and I can't see." (She placed her head on her desk, tightened her shoulder muscles, and began sobbing.) "He's crushing my body. I'm smothering. I can't breathe." It took a little while for her to realize she was in the classroom and safe.

Sometimes a child tells her mother about the incest and her mother doesn't believe her – or believes, but blames, her. This further traumatizes the child, creating within her the belief that she was a victimizer – not a victim. The mother, in this latter instance, protects her own needs instead of the child's.

Anna's uncle (mother's brother) incested Anna when she was a small child and again when she was 10 or 11. Still the mother sent her to live with that uncle for a while. Anna protested, "but he raped (she didn't know the word 'incest') me." Her mother's response was "he has a girlfriend now, so he doesn't need you in that way anymore."

Later, when this same pre-teen was molested by a neighbor, her mother punished her for going near the neighbor, only adding to her trauma.

ometimes the child doesn't have the language to report incest. One woman told me that she reported incest to her mother in her pre-school-aged vocabulary:

"Daddy bothers me."

Her mother, failing to understand the child's need, replied, "Ignore him. He's just teasing you."

Sometimes the incested child runs away from home, but police find her and return her to her family, thus allowing the trauma to continue.

One woman told me that, after being incested as a child, the perpetrator gifted her, perhaps as a way to keep the incest unreported. Another told me that three of her mother's brothers "would put me on the mantle when I was small and touch and lick my 'guche' (vagina) and give me money for it."

This placed the child in an ambivalent state, creating conflicting emotions within her. She wanted the money gift (which she interpreted as love) but not the incest (which she perceived as pain). However, to receive the gift, she had to accept the incest. When a family member alternately loves/ punishes a child, confusion and ambivalence result.

Women in my classes, sexually molested as children, reported experiencing themselves as helpless victims. They then gravitated to drugs to numb their feelings and/or to unhealthy relationships to avoid being alone. Many wounded incarcerated women have told me, "I would prefer to be in an abusive relationship than to be alone (helpless)".

It is highly unlikely that a healthy mature woman would make a similar relationship choice.

Gina's father incested her and her sister when their mother was hospitalized following the birth of a baby. He incested a neighbor child too. Gina's mother did not believe her daughters. However, the neighbor pressed charges, and police arrested him.

Another woman, Maiya, about 25, told me that her mother died when Maiya was very young. Her father moved the family of four children from a northwest state to Missouri. The children stayed with Aunt Bev and Uncle Bull while their father found work in a nearby state.

Over the years, Maiya grew close to Uncle Bull. He bought old, run-down homes and, together, they rehabbed them. She loved the work and basked in Uncle Bull's attention and affirmation of her.

When she was a young teen, she injured someone while defending her cousin from a gang. Uncle Bull "took the rap" for her.

After Uncle Bull's release from jail, he incested Maiya whenever he was intoxicated. Maiya allowed the incest, believing that she owed it to him for saving her from juvenile detention.

Words tell us something about ourselves. Active tense verbs have a stronger impact than passive tense verbs. You have, no doubt, noticed that I changed the noun "incest" to the verb "incested" in several chapters. That may have made you uncomfortable. But why?

Why do we find it easy to say a person "burglarized, shop-lifted, cheated, robbed, drugged, stabbed, raped, murdered" a victim but we feel uncomfortable saying "he incested her?"

I choose, like many of my therapist friends, to change the noun 'incest' into a verb. This removes any uncertainty that the child or the teen "brought it on herself," or that the act was voluntary, and clarifies that she is a victim, not a co-aggressor in the act.

Incest is so repugnant – so disgusting to our sensibilities – that we pretend it doesn't happen. Victims of incest are usually children and young teens. They sometimes blame themselves for these assaults to their sexuality and their psyches.

Fortunately, all traumatic symptoms, including those of incest, can be healed and transformed.

> Trauma is a fact of life. It does not, however, have to be a life sentence. Not only can trauma be healed, but with appropriate guidance and support, it can be transformative. Trauma has the potential to be one of the most significant forces for psychological, social, and spiritual awakening and evolution.
>
> (Peter A. Levine, PhD. Op. Cit.)

If you ever saw a deer or other animal – bruised but not seriously injured – after being grazed by a car, you may have noticed how its body shook for several seconds before it recovered, got up and scampered off into the woods. It didn't stop to think "What just happened?" or "What do I do next?" Its instincts took over and shook off the trauma.

But humans are "wired" differently. Instead of letting our instincts take over and shake us out of a traumatic freeze response, our human brains try to think our way through the aftermath of painful events. The trapped trauma energies then get imprinted into our nervous system.

I personally experienced a woman in my class shake off her trauma. J'Aulian, a 30'ish woman, told me that neighbors wrongfully accused her of abusing her children. As a result, The Department of Family Services (DFS) took the children and placed them in its care. After a few weeks, the DFS reported to J'Aulian's jail case worker that they saw no indication of abuse in the children. With great jubilation, J'Aulian reported her wonderful news to the class. She thought the DFS would return the children to her, and she would be released from jail.

However, a few days later, authorities told her that the prosecutor, disregarding the DFS's "no abuse" findings, decided to let the child abuse charge stand.

J'Aulian's distress during the next class, seemed unbearable. Her screams and sobs resembled a freight train barreling through the space. Holding the other students' attention was impossible.

Instead, while the other seven women sat silently waiting and watching, I wrapped J'Aulain in my arms and held her for what seemed like several minutes, while her heart emptied out its pain. Eventually, as I continued to hold her, her body shook violently for at least five minutes.

Then an unexpected thing happened. Suddenly, her screams and bodily tremors stopped.

I could hardly believe my eyes when, almost immediately thereafter, she sat up straight and entered fully into the remainder of the class, even laughing, at times, with the group.

Reflecting, later, on the experience, I feel certain that she went through the "animal response" to trauma, and that her shaking and tremors discharged the trapped energies that had piled up in her body. She was free.

After that class, she was able to report, without "falling apart", a series of previous traumas. They included 15 years of molestation, being unwanted by her mother, and the deaths of two of her other children.

She completed the remaining classes of the course and did excellent work on her papers.

Because J'aulian's case was heard in Family Court, I was unable to be present and do not know how it ended. My hope is that she regained custody of her children and that she and her children are now doing well.

See the stories of Leisha and Mattie in the following chapters.

CHAPTER SEVENTEEN:
LEISHA

INCEST and BODY DYSMORPHIA

*L*eisha was born into a multi-cultural, bi-racial family. The inter-family relationships are complicated, but I will try to simplify them. Family members are:

Magda: Leisha's birth mother who was of East European descent. Magda had a severe drug problem at the time of Leisha's birth and early years. She spent time in prison.

Dino: Leisha's birth father. Dino's mother was a woman of color and his father, bi-racial. Dino's parents divorced and he lived with his mother during his young years. Dino had a drug problem and was in prison when Leisha was born.

Jerry is Dino's birth father; Leisha's grandfather. He was a lawyer. With Dino in prison, Jerry became Leisha's adoptive father.

Leona was Jerry's wife and became Leisha's adoptive mother.

Jerry and Leona divorced when Leisha was three years old. Leona raised her, but Jerry continued to play an active grandfather role in her young life. It was Leona who shared much of Leisha's life story with me.

In this story, Leisha refers to her grandparents, Jerry and Leona, as dad and mom. She refers to her birth parents, Magda and Dino, by their given names.

Leisha's <u>written</u> story is short, reflecting her minimalist speaking pattern. She offered much more information during interviews. I incorporated the interview data into her written words. At Leisha's request I spent several hours with Leona and integrated the data Leona gave me into Leisha's story.

Although she was 40 when she wrote her story, Leisha's voice was high and thin, sounding much like a child of 10 or 11. She was about five feet tall and weighed close to 200 pounds. She hated her body.

IN LEISHA'S WORDS

"0-6 months: back and forth between biological mother and adoptive parents, all of whom lived in Chicago.

"Six months to three years – lived with adoptive parents. Dad was an accomplished lawyer. Mom held a governmental position.

"Age three to the present – lived with mom (Leona). Mom and dad had divorced. Mom tells me that, at six months, Magda summoned her to come and get me. Mom discovered Magda zonked out. She found me rocking in a closet amongst a pile of clothes, malnourished and diaper-less. So, like my birth parents, I suffered from early abandonment issues. I would cling to mom for dear life. I slept with mom until I was 14. (Leona volunteered the information that Leisha's bedding with Leona for all of those years was one of the reasons Jerry divorced her.)

"I was a good kid, a very solemn child: studied piano, ballet and went to private schools.

Dino was around occasionally, for holidays, but spent most of my childhood in and out of prison despite the fact that dad, his birth father, was an accomplished attorney.

"Mom and dad divorced when I was three and I would see dad every weekend. He would pick me up and cart me around everywhere. I always had a 'kiddie cocktail' when I was with him. He was a functional alcoholic. He has a glass of wine in his hand in every picture I have of him. He was a fun-loving, 'life is a bowl of cherries', kind of guy.

"Mom had an important position in a federal agency. She worked hard and long hours and succeeded on her journey up the proverbial ladder before her retirement. Mom and dad stressed the 'lady-like, good girl' way of life. No sadness or anger allowed. I still struggle to express those feelings."

Sometime after her retirement from the governmental agency – Leisha was in her early 20's by this time – Leona moved Leisha and herself from Chicago to St. Louis.

"Around puberty, age 11 or so, Dino started molesting me. He would photograph and film me naked. I am still ashamed of my body and hate to see myself unclothed. This is, incidentally, about the same time I started smoking pot (marijuana) and drinking beer. Dino gave me pot.

"Although I became sexually active with my boyfriend in high school, and smoked marijuana frequently, I was a good student. I maintained an A average and had the highest ACT test scores in the school's history.

"At age 15, I was raped and beaten by two adult males. I was sexually abused by every male I encountered in childhood from the baby- sitter's kids to my male cousins. I was almost raped, at the age of 10, by a gang of kids forcing one boy to attack me."

"I have survived molestation, drugs, cancer and jail. I am a survivor."

Leola shared her experience of Magda's abandonment of Leisha. "If you don't come and get this baby, I may hurt her," Magda told Leona on the phone.

Leona rushed to Magda's apartment. "I knocked on the front door several times and Magda didn't respond. I went around to the back and knocked on that door several times too. I called Magda's name, but she didn't come."

Leona's imagination ran wild causing her to be frantic. She returned to the front door and pounded on it. "Finally, Magda came to the door, but she was totally 'out of it' as she climbed the stairs and fell asleep on the bed."

Leisha was nowhere in sight. "I was so afraid," Leona said. "I went from room to room and opened every door looking for the baby. Finally, I found her, diaper-less, sitting on a pile of dirty clothes, thumb in mouth, and rocking in the closet. I looked for clean clothing, but all I could find were one shoe and a coat."

Leona wrapped the baby in her own outer wear to ward off the winter cold, left Magda asleep on the bed, and took the baby home. Leona's neighbor bathed Leisha while Leona shopped for diapers and clothing.

When she returned home, Leona gathered the baby in her arms and took her to a pediatrician. "He wanted to report Magda to authorities for neglect, because Leisha was so malnourished. But I talked him out of it, knowing that Leisha was now safe."

Researchers tell us that, although we don't develop the necessary brain organs to remember pre-three-year-old emotional experiences, the energy of those events embed themselves in our body cells. It disturbs one's consciousness to visualize what the pain of Leisha's cells felt like to this baby who had no way to express those feelings except to suck her thumb and rock back and forth on the closet floor. My image is of maggots squirming in the baby's cells, sucking every vestige of safety and security out of her tiny body.

According to Leona, "Leisha rocked and sucked her thumb for a long time, and she didn't smile."

Leona tried to stay in touch with Magda during the first year of Leisha's life. "Once I went to the club to see Magda dance. She was stripping. She looked at the audience, saw me, and was very embarrassed. I never went back."

"When it became clear that Magda was incapable of caring for Leisha, Leona and her husband, Jerry, adopted the child. However, they divorced when Leisha was three and Leisha stayed with Leona although, as Leisha said in her story, Jerry remained active in her life.

Leona travelled a lot with her government job and Leisha stayed with a baby-sitter.

Violations of Leisha's sexuality began early in her life and continued into her teen years. She didn't tell Leola when, as a young child, she was raped by the baby-sitter's son. When I asked why, Leisha said, "I don't know. Probably because I was an only child and didn't want the baby-sitter to go away."

Leona told Leisha early in life that she was adopted. However, Leisha said she didn't realize, until age 11, that Dino was her birth father. She thought he was her brother.

I asked why she didn't tell Leona that Dino incested her and photographed her naked. Her response was: "my boundaries have been so messed up for so long that I don't know if I thought it was wrong."

The molestation continued until she "grew up enough to tell him to get the hell away from me...and not to touch me again." She estimated her age, at that time, to have been about 14 or 15 and said, "after I laid the law down to him, he abided by it."

According to Leona, Dino's birth mother had warned her not to let Leisha be alone with Dino because "he has a problem." However, Leona could not supervise Leisha's activities round-the-clock between the years of 11-15 when he was molesting her.

Once the incest began, Leisha became "a disturbance maker, blurting out answers" in class. "I would finish my work and become bored."

She also began "smoking pot" that Dino gave her "and drinking beer."

Leisha's behavior apparently annoyed her teachers too, so Leona transferred her to a private school. Leisha loved this school but apparently drugs were readily available there, and her drug use progressed rapidly to LSD and mushrooms (hallucinatory drugs), speed, black beauties, yellow jackets (Nembutals) and red devils' (Seconals), the latter two being sleeping pills. (Women in my classes have told me that they like methamphetamines which can keep them awake for days. They then take heroin or sedatives - sleeping pills - to bring them down from the meth induced highs.)

"My mom was so protective, after she discovered this stuff, she sent me off to another school where I had way more access to drugs than previously."

The Rape, Abuse & Incest National Network (RAINN), reports that "the effects of child sexual abuse can be long-lasting and affect the victim's mental health. Victims are more likely than non-victims to experience the following mental health challenges:

- About 4 times more likely to develop symptoms of drug abuse,
- About 4 times more likely to experience PTSD as adults,
- About 3 times more likely to experience a major depressive episode as adults.

Leisha's diagnoses include posttraumatic stress disorder (PTSD), depression, anxiety disorder, and dysmorphia (a distaste for one's own body - some-times known as dysmorphophobia). She has prescriptions for a wide variety of drugs to control her symptoms. Because she finds it difficult to maintain interest in anything for any length of time, she believes she needs to be tested for adult attention deficit disorder (AADD).

Why is incest so likely to cause psychological problems?

> ... an incestual relationship involves a betrayal of the victim by someone she should implicitly trust. A person who is responsible to protect the child and keep her safe from danger becomes the danger. The watch dog becomes the attack dog."
>
> (Jennifer J. Freyd. *Betrayal Trauma: The Logic of Forgetting Childhood Abuse*. Harvard university Press, 2008.)

In addition to PTSD, depression, anxiety disorder, and dysmorphophobia, Leisha has twice suffered from breast cancer. At age 29, she felt a pea-sized lump in one breast. Two months later it was removed and, "at the time of removal, had grown to the size of a plumb and entered my lymph system".

Leisha then went into drug treatment and stopped using illegal drugs.

Seven years later, cancer recurred in the same spot. A radical mastectomy and more chemo-therapy followed. Leisha developed Bell's Palsy which lasted four months. She again began using illegal drugs. About these traumatic times, she said, "I could only eat popsicles. I was always nauseated."

During those 18 months, Leisha took prescribed steroids and "went heavily into drugs." When "I came out of the drug induced stupor, I weighed 298 pounds. It was like someone put a helium spout in my mouth and I just blew up."

At her one-year checkup following her second bout with cancer, Leisha had a cyst under the scar. The surgeon excised it but it "left a hole in my chest about the size of a half dollar. The hole tunneled through my chest."

The surgeon attempted to repair the damage but a week later, the tissue began to necrose, that is, to die. Eventually a plastic surgeon repaired the damage.

Dr. Carolyn Myss, medical intuitive, and author of several books including *Anatomy of the Spirit* and *Why People Don't Heal and How They Can*, writes about illnesses as related to the body's energy centers or chakras. "Breast cancer," she wrote, "is caused by a disturbance in the energy flow in [the] heart chakra.

> (Carolyn Myss PhD. *Why People Don't Heal and How They Can*. New York: Three Rivers Press, Member of Crown Publishing Co., 1977).

If this is true, Leisha's refusal to nourish herself is not necessarily conscious. Neither Leona nor her ex-husband, Jerry, allowed expressions of anger or sadness which are some of the ways people respond to pain. As Leisha said, at age 40, "I am still struggling to express these feelings."

Also significant are her relationships with her birth parents, Magda and Dino.

About Magda, Leisha said "she is now clean of drugs, married and lives on the west coast. She has three other children and I've met all of them. Every ten years or so Magda has a burning desire to see or talk with me."

Leisha said that Dino, too, is now drug free and holds a good job. He still lives in Illinois, is divorced from his third wife, and has fathered six children in addition to Leisha. Every six months or so, Leisha visits Dino, or he travels to St. Louis to visit her. She added "after he was clean for a couple of years, he sent me off to an elaborate place in Arizona for treatment. They had really good programs there, including programs for sexual molestation, but he only enrolled me in the co-dependency program."

Through the 14 hours that Leisha attended my classes, I saw her intent on learning. But I never saw her smile. Likewise, she seemed totally cerebral – no smiles and no emotion as she told me about Dino's goodness.

I asked, "Do you have ambivalent feelings about Dino?"

"I've forgiven him," she responded, "because he's a different person now than he was then, but yes, I have lots of ambivalence. I respect him as a human being – he's now a father figure: supportive, very remorseful and he does everything in his power to make amends."

Questions about his amends remain, however. Why, when he paid for her to go to "the elaborate place in Arizona" for treatment, did he enroll her in a co-dependency program instead of a program to deal with his incesting of her? Was this action more self-serving and protective of himself than therapy for her?

Leisha continued, "[Dino's] greatest gift to me is that he's a father to his other children, my half-siblings. To my knowledge he never molested any of them".

Still the contrasts between Leisha and her birth parents seem significant. Dino, the father perpetrator, is doing well in terms of being drug and prison-free. He holds a good job, makes a living wage, and has a positive relationship with his other children.'

Likewise, Magda is drug-free, out of prison, and is reported as having a close relationship with her other three children.

Leisha, on the other hand, now 46 years old, continues to struggle with the aftermath of breast cancer and body dysmorphia, and "cannot stand to look at my body".

At the time of this writing, she has completed seven years of parole. This parole followed her imprisonment which resulted when Leona called the police to arrest her. Leisha, high on drugs, had physically wrestled Leona, in Leona's driveway, to steal her purse and car keys.

Leona, Leisha's adopted mother, is in her late-eighties at the time of this writing. She lives alone and is in failing health. A hired woman performs her household chores, including cleaning, laundry, and grocery shopping. Leona rarely leaves her home except when, on occasion, the housekeeper drives her to a restaurant for lunch.

Because she has been the primary victim of Leisha's prior crimes of stealing and forging checks (and, Leona added, Leisha once sneaked a man into my [Leona's] basement without my knowledge), Leona no longer allows Leisha to enter her home. She has placed bars on all her windows and doors to prevent her daughter from gaining entrance.

Leona is caught in the bind of needing to protect herself from Leisha's intrusions and, at the same time, wanting to help Leisha become independent post-prison. As a compromise, Leona set up an apartment for Leisha's use and bought her a car. But now, Leisha must support herself for the first time in her life.

Leisha's life began as a neglected baby. Incest and rape invaded her preteen and teen years. Radiation, chemotherapy and two periods of breast cancer, followed by surgical complications, kept her homebound and almost bedfast for 18 months. She coped by increasing the drug use. Crime and prison followed.

She, who suffered from malnutrition and abandonment in her early years, has survived much. But the question remains: What will it take for her to nourish herself and to thrive *as an adult*?

CHAPTER EIGHTEEN:
MATTIE

SOCIALIZED, THROUGH PLAY, INTO INCEST

Mattie wrote part of her story for me. However, she shared more in verbal conversations. I have incorporated this latter verbal material into her written story.

IN MATTIE'S WORDS

"My name is Mattie. I am 43 years old. My father was a sharecropper in Mississippi and a deacon in a church in Angola, MS. He died of sickle cell anemia at age 43. I was six or seven when he died. My mother grew me and my brother and younger sister up (raised us as a single parent). Later in life I learned that my mother had another child when she was 14. She sometimes visited us in Mississippi, but she was 20 years older than I, and I didn't realize she was my sister until we lived in St. Louis. We were born in Mississippi but raised in the state of Missouri. This change of address took place after the death of my father.

"In Mississippi, we were sharecroppers. We were very poor and lived in a shack on a white man's plantation. I could look through the floor and see the ground and snakes and earthworms and stuff like that underneath the house. And in the wintertime, it was real cold in the house. I remember my father slaughtering hogs and my mother wringing chickens' necks for the plantation owner.

"After my father died, my mother moved us to St. Louis where her mother and sister lived.

"I'm currently living in a house with my mother, daughter and older brother, but our lives are separate. My mother lives mostly in her room. She is very sick. My brother also lives mostly in his room. My daughter and I mostly live outside the home. Even though we live in my mom's house we are almost never there.

"Each one of us lives our lives separately, for our own different reasons. My brother and I are always in conflict with one another. My mother is off to herself and her religion. My daughter and I are being distant from each other, because I am totally selfishly involved with my significant other and the drugs I use.

"My childhood was like my daughter's, because I was distant from my mother also. My mother used to drink when I was a child growing up. She would leave us – my brother, sister and me – on weekends. She would go to her sister's house in University City. She wanted us to go with her, but we weren't interested.

"Before she got sick, my mother was a good provider. She worked at a toy company. When that company went out of business, she cleaned peoples' houses. She just wasn't there for me as a friend or someone I could con-fide in. As a result of not being able to confide in her, I didn't tell her about being molested when I was a child. I became a distant child and was very stand-offish growing up.

"The first boy I ever got close to, I married at age seventeen. My mother insisted that if I was going to have relations with a boy, I would have to marry him. She took us to her church, and we got married. When I became preg-nant, my classmates started looking down on me and so I stopped going to school in the 10th grade. I restarted school three times but never finished.

"Then I had a miscarriage. I felt depressed and started using drugs".

MATTIE'S SEXUAL/MOLESTATION HISTORY

"When I was three or four, my cousins and I played 'catch a girl, kiss a girl.' My older cousins would do certain things. They would feel you or whatever and grab you and roll against you and stuff. It didn't feel right to me. I was uncomfortable with that.

"Then, my grandfather came and stayed with us in St. Louis. He was blind, and we used to play with him all the time. We liked the idea that he was getting up and getting after us...and having to fumble his way to finding us by listening for our voices.

"He'd say 'I'm gonna' get you kids,' so we would run and stand up against the wall, and he'd come straight to us like he could see us, and he would hit us with his stick.

"One time he caught me and had me layin' on top of him, and he was holding onto me real tight and, you know, I remember I was wet and I was looking at this white stuff he squirted on me, and I was, like, 'oh, God!'

"He did this more than once. And I remember the feeling that I felt when he did this, and I didn't like his holding me down like he was. I didn't like the feeling of being restrained. I was feeling – I don't know – as it was happening - it was a feeling like it wasn't right. I remember feeling like I was dirty. That put a lot of shame feelings in me too.

"After my grandfather, my brother took it up. And then my mother had a man that came with his three daughters and stayed with us, and one of his daughters started messing with us. This girl was naked. My brother held her up, and her legs were open, and I was screaming 'she's got a hole', you know, in her privates, and we all thought that was strange. My sister told my mother, and my mother got mad and threw a lamp and made the man leave.

"Then my brother began molesting me. He was three years older than me. We molested each other. I thought this was the way people played house.

"When I was a teen, my aunt's boyfriend fondled us when we were in bed.

"When I was in my late twenties or early thirties, I was raped at gunpoint while I was using drugs. I had gone to a neighborhood to prostitute. The man forced me into his car, held a gun to my head and then took me to an alley and repeatedly raped me. I tried to sweettalk him. I said 'if this was what you wanted, why didn't you just ask for it. I'd have given it to you. You didn't have to have a gun.'

"Apparently, I convinced him because he let me go to make a phone call. I went into a store and two guys I knew came in. They shielded me to help me get away from the guy with the gun."

MATTIE'S PHYSICAL PROBLEMS

Mattie reported that she has trichomoniasis, a sexually transmitted disease, in addition to a benign tumor in her uterus. She learned about the presence of the tumor when she was pregnant with her youngest daughter, but she has not seen a doctor about it. In addition, the sweat glands under her arms give her trouble. The keloids are inflamed and drain.

MATTIE'S PREGNANCY HISTORY

Over a period of 20 years, Mattie birthed 14 children.

After the miscarriage, she birthed three additional sons with the man she married at age 17. When her third son was born, Mattie and her husband partially separated, and Mattie moved in with her mother.

"My older sister was telling me 'I think you better get ready to go — too many kids in the house'. I remember that I felt isolated, me and my kids.

"For a whole year after my third child's birth and my separation from my husband, I couldn't eat or sleep. I lost weight. My sister kept saying 'you gotta' come out of this — you gotta' come out of this.' So I started goin' out with her to clubs and stuff. And I took up with the first man told me I ain't ugly. My husband couldn't believe this. I cut all ties with him when our third child was three years old."

Mattie did not tell me what happened to those three children. She didn't speak of them again, so her ex-husband may have taken them with him.

With a second man, after her divorce from her husband, Mattie had a miscarriage, an abortion and three children (two boys and a girl) whom she "adopted out."

With a third man, she had a son whom she "adopted out". This man, she said, was a drug dealer.

She doesn't know who fathered her next child, a girl, whom she also gave for adoption because she (Mattie) was homeless and prostituting when she became pregnant.

With a fourth man, Mattie had a daughter, followed by a son, both of whom she gave for adoption. With this same man, she had another daughter who is the one in Mattie's life today.

Mattie participated fully in *Becoming All We Can Be*, the course I created and taught in the jail. As the course proceeded, it become obvious that she had never been introduced to the concept of personal dignity. It had never occurred to her that her life was worthwhile and that she could take control of her life and make decisions to better herself.

"All my life," Mattie said, "I felt like I needed men in my life to strengthen me. Now I feel like my strength is building inside me."

In class, Mattie identified her addictions as alcohol, men and sex.

Her face lit up in the 7th class, when she learned about the eight kinds of intelligence, including Naturalist Intelligence. She shared that, since childhood, she has loved nature, exploring grasses and ant hills to see where the ants were going. "I used to put my ears on the ground and listen for the worms crawling underneath," she said. "I think I'd like to work with the earth."

MATTIE'S DRUG AND INCARCERATION HISTORY

Mattie's brother-in-law introduced her to marijuana when she was 16. At age 24, she used PCP (an hallucinogen) and, at age 28, her younger sister introduced her to crack cocaine. She became addicted to crack and stopped using other drugs. Later, when she was about 42, she used heroin for seven months, but she has been drug-free since that time (about a year).

Mattie's incarcerations have resulted from her relationships with boyfriends. In the first instance, a boyfriend made her go to Dillard's Department Store with him. He "popped open some crystal glasses" and made Mattie steal them. (Women hide shop-lifted items in their purses and pockets, under their dresses and in their bras, jeans and underpants. One woman told me she once hid a whole ham in her underpants. Others sneak out of the store with the items in a cart). Mattie thought someone had seen her take the crystal glasses, so she went to a police officer and turned herself in. She did this to keep her boyfriend from getting caught. In court the judge placed her on probation.

The second incident occurred when the friend of a boyfriend "stole suits and got caught". He implicated Mattie because she was in the car with him. The judge sentenced her to five-years- probation plus restitution.

When Mattie had a visit with her probation officer, the PO told her she needed to finish paying restitution. Mattie thought she had paid restitution in full, so she didn't pay any more. She was placed in jail for six months because of this misunderstanding. This is when I met her.

Mattie was born in rural Mississippi. Her parents were poor sharecroppers. It is possible that stimulation of children's genitalia was a parental practice in that area of rural America in the 1960's when she was born.

A significant difference exists, however, between those practices to calm babies and what Mattie's blind grandfather did to her. His actions were performed to pleasure himself. In fact, even at her young age, it seemed repulsive to her. The childhood practices, identified in articles, about sooth- ing crying babies, were performed for the sake of the babies or small chil- dren – to comfort them, to help them sleep. On the other hand, Mattie's grandfather acted to pleasure himself.

Some of the actions of her older brother seemed innocent – they thought it was the way one played house. However, other actions of her brother and her older cousins seem clearly to have been incest.

The question is: what effect did these incestual relationships have on Mattie? It is impossible, I suspect, to answer that question without also addressing the family's poverty and educational level.

What we do know is that she prostituted to finance herself and, over a period of 20 years, had 14 pregnancies by four men. Apparently, she did not use, or did not have access to, contraceptives. Otherwise, it seems she would have used them since she aborted one baby and offered seven others for adoption. (On the other hand, I have had women in my classes who have told me that they were not "in a position" to raise children but did not use contraceptives when they had sex because their church forbade use of them). Perhaps Mattie was one of these women.

Earlier in this book, we learned that women, incested as children, were caught in a freeze situation when they could neither run away from, nor fight their abuser. These children often grow up feeling helpless and hope-less about their lives. This seems to have been the case with Mattie.

However, hope exists for her in the fact that one of her last statements to me was: "All my life I felt I needed men to strengthen me. But my strength is building, and I don't feel that way anymore."

CHAPTER NINETEEN: PROSTITUTION AND THE SEX INDUSTRY

Once upon a time, there was a naïve belief that legalized prostitution would improve life for prostitutes, eliminate prostitution in areas where it remained illegal and remove organized crime from the business. As founder and co-chair of the Congressional Human Trafficking Caucus, I know that like all fairy tales, this turns out to be sheer fantasy.

(Congresswoman Carolyn Maloney in the Forward to Melissa Farley. *Prostitution & Trafficking in Nevada: Making the Connections.* Prostitution Research and Education P.O. Box 16254. San Francisco, CA 94116- 0254. 2007).

*T*he word "prostitution" did not exist in my childhood vocabulary. In my upper teen and college days, people in my life's sphere occasionally mentioned the "Red Light District" but, to my knowledge, I never met anyone involved in prostitution. They existed, in my mind, on the fringes of society – somewhere near the bottom rung of humanity. Never having met a woman who told me she prostituted, I never had occasion to ask why. I simply presumed they were "oversexed" with lives lacking a moral under-girding.

Today the situation is quite different. Almost every woman who enrolls in my course, in the jail, shares in one way or another, that she prostitutes.

Few people dispute the fact that, despite decades of feminist work to promote sex/gender equality, and despite many improvements in women's position in society, women continue to be valued less than men. This carries into the sex industry as well as in other areas of life.

In her book, SLUT, Leora Tanenbaum identifies the differences in the way society portrays women who prostitute as compared to the men (johns) who hire them:

> Positive expressions for a Sexually Active man: stud, player, stallion, ladies' man, Romeo, Don Juan, Casanova, bounder, gigolo, lover, lover man/boy.
>
> Positive expressions for a sexually active woman: hot, sexy.
>
> Negative expressions for a sexually active man: womanizer, wolf, can't keep it in his pants.
>
> Negative expressions for a sexually active woman: slut, whore, tramp, ho, bitch, hoochie mama, pig, prostitute, hooker, nympho, harlot, hussy, tart, bimbo, floozy, vixen, minx, loose woman, fallen woman.
>
> (Leora Tanenbaum. *SLUT*. New York: Seven Stories Press. 1999).

This difference plays out in the minds of many men who engage prostitutes too.

Most of the women in my classes volunteer that they prostitute to support their families or their addictions. They see it as a necessity. However in jail, as in general society, differing attitudes toward prostitution abound.

"I have principles," Jancine told our class. "I don't prostitute and I don't sell drugs to kids."

Another woman, Carmen, said, "Wealthy families might give a diamond ring to a young girl as a legacy. But I came from a poor family. My family didn't want me to prostitute like my mother, so my granny and my brothers saved me from that. They taught me to shoplift. Shoplifting was my family's legacy to me."

Incarcerated women, themselves, have varying opinions about prostitution. For example, two women argued one morning as they walked into the classroom. I overheard one of them insist loudly, "I am NOT a prostitute. I'm a Call Girl."

They moved into chairs on opposite sides of the group and the second woman asked me, "Do you know the difference between a prostitute and a call girl?"

I didn't at the time, so I responded "no."

She enlightened me: "$200."

Women prostitute for a variety of reasons:
- forced into prostitution by a relative,
- supplement their income so they can feed and clothe themselves and/or their families,
- forced into trafficking: These are often, but not always, runaway youth, refugees or immigrants, enticed by offers of a good life, only to find themselves in bondage,
- to feed a drug addiction,
- to satisfy a sex addiction,
- to pay college expenses and/or repay student loans.

Let's look, more fully, at each of these reasons.

FORCED INTO PROSTITUTION BY A RELATIVE. You read, in a previous chapter, about Delila whose mother sent her to pick up a package, which unbeknownst to Delila contained drugs.

The dealer forced Delila into a one-time rape situation in payment for the drugs.

PROSTITUTION TO SUPPLEMENT INCOME.

Mona's husband required her to prostitute to earn extra money for the family.

Pre-teens and teens (11-15) running away from abuse at home are too young to qualify for a legal job. If they do not find organizations like Covenant House to shelter them, they enter prostitution. Sexual activity is usually not new to them. It is what happened to them in their home and what they ran away from. You have read previous stories in this book about women who, as children/pre-teens, entered prostitution after running from parental abuse.

Mature women enter prostitution to supplement their incomes too. Miss Jefferson, a woman, in her late 30's or early 40's who came one day to my class at the jail refused to focus on the day's topic for discussion. Over and over, she redirected the class with statements like "Prostitutes make great money. Prostitution is a terrific way of life. We should legalize prostitution."

Time and again, I asked her to focus on the class topic, but she refused. Eventually I took her aside and suggested that, because she found it impossible to focus on the designated topic, she leave class and return to her cell. So, she did.

At the end of the class, Miss Mel, a Correctional Officer (CO), called me aside and advocated for the woman. The officer said something like this: "You might not know that Miss Jefferson is a single mother with five children. She also has financial responsibility for her wheelchair bound sister and her sister's two children. She prostitutes to keep all of them clothed and fed".

I felt stunned, but certainly wiser.

Miss Jefferson came to the next class with a note of apology for interrupting the class.

That humbling encounter opened my eyes. Adult education should meet the student where she is and build from there. Otherwise, we simply mouth information instead of helping students learn. It would probably have been freeing and healing for all the women, had I allowed them to talk openly about prostitution for a while before returning to the topic for the day's discussion. Their conversation would definitely have been educational for me.

Sadie, a large woman of about 55 years, spent several years as secretary for a variety of companies. Her bosses, in each of those companies, gave their hands unwanted access to her large breasts and buttocks. Sadie relieved herself of her victimization by becoming her own boss. She set up an Escort Service and became a Madam in the business. It worked for a few years.

However, police eventually arrested her, and brought her to jail for operating a business without a license.

TRAFFICKED CHILDREN/TEENS/YOUNG WOMEN: Much news today focuses on trafficking of children and women. Many organizations try to help them. Some of the trafficked people are kidnapped children and teens.

In their book, *Renting Lucy: A Story of America's Prostituted Children*, Linda Smith with Cindy Coloma, explain that these children are often runaways: teens, pre-teens, immigrants and refugees. Enticed by internet offers of lucrative careers, the young women are unwittingly lured into the harem (sometimes called stables) of a pimp (person who organizes a group of women into prostitution, collects their earnings and provides protection for them). Sometimes the pimps are teams of men and women working together. The amount of money paid the trafficked woman is insufficient for her to escape the pimp's control.

> (Linda Smith with Cindy Coloma. *Renting Lucy: A Story of America's Prostituted Children*. Vancouver, WA: Shared Hope International, 2009).

Trafficking is a world-wide problem.

> In 2013, human trafficking was about a $32 billion industry across the world. In 2017, it was $152 billion. It's the second-fastest-growing crime in the world, surpassed only by gun [crimes]. [In the United States] calls to the [National Human Trafficking] hotline have more than doubled in the last five years.

> (Dawn Araugo-Hawkins, *Q & A with Sr. Jeanne Christensen, RSM, on how anti-trafficking work has evolved. Sisters Global Report: A Project of National Catholic Reporter*. February 8, 2018).

The problem of human trafficking was addressed, in the early part of this century, by the United Nations. Known as the *Palermo Protocol to Prevent, Suppress and Punish Trafficking in Persons, especially Women and Children*, it was ratified in 2000 and entered into force on 25 December, 2003. As of February 2018, it had been ratified by 173 parties including the United States of America.

The Palermo Protocol against Trafficking is one of three protocols adopted by the United Nations to supplement the 2000 Convention against Transnational Organized Crime. Article 3 of the Palermo Protocol against Trafficking defines trafficking as:

> The recruitment, transportation, transfer, harboring or receipt of persons, by means of threat or use of force or other forms of coercion, of abduction, of fraud, of deception, of the abuse of power or of a position of vulnerability or the giving or receiving of payments or benefits to achieve the consent of a person having control over another person, for the purpose of exploitation. Exploitation shall include, at a minimum, the exploitation or the prostitution of others, or other forms of exploitation, forced labor or services, slavery, or practices similar to slavery, servitude or the removal of organs.

Each country can opt to translate the Protocol into its legislation. The United States congress named its adaptation the "*Trafficking Victims Protection Act* (TVPA)." It defines trafficking as:

> a) a commercial sex act induced by force, fraud or coercion, or in which the person induced to perform such act has not attained 18 years of age; or

> b) the recruitment, harboring, transportation, provision, or obtaining of a person for labor or services, through the use of force, fraud, or coercion, for the purpose of subjection to involuntary servitude, peonage, debt bondage, or slavery."

Part a) of the TVPA refers, of course to trafficking for the purpose of prostitution while Part b) refers to trafficking for the purpose of occupational labor. A myth about trafficking is that the majority of people trafficked in the United States are imported from other countries. That is a misconception.

> The concept of sex trafficked people as only those from other countries trafficked into the United States is problematic...Research shows that U.S. citizens comprise the majority of Sex Trafficked People in the United States.

> (Farrell et al 2012; Martin et al, 2014, US Dept. of State 2014 reported on page 8 of Andrea J. Nichols. *Sex Trafficking in the United States: Theory, Research, Practice, Policy and Practice.* New York: Columbia University Press. 2016).

The United States considers every child or teen under 18 who is enticed into prostitution, whether voluntarily or by force, to be a victim of trafficking.

Several anti-trafficking organizations have been set up in the United States and across the world to help citizens recognize signs of trafficked children and women. These focus primarily on truck stops, bus stations, hotels where conventions are held, sports arenas, and hospital emergency rooms where trafficking victims may be taken for treatment of injuries they have sustained.

PROSTITUTING TO OBTAIN MONEY FOR DRUGS: The majority of women in my jail course have drug addictions secondary to the traumas experienced in their childhood/teen years. Being too young to legally obtain a job, they prostitute to obtain money for drugs. You have read some of their stories in the previous chapters.

SEX ADDICTIONS:

> Like other addictions, sexual addiction is a progressive disorder. Psychologist Patrick Carnes, Ph.D. names three levels of sexual addiction beginning with compulsive masturbation to exhibitionism/voyeurism and finally to child molestation, incest and rape.
> (Patrick Carnes, Ph.D. *Out of the Shadows: Understanding Sexual Addiction*. Center City, MN: Hazeldon, Third Edition. 2001).

It is probable that the men and women – termed pedophiles – who incested the children whose stories appear in this book, would be classified as having sexual addictions. My course in the jail does not address sexuality directly. Nevertheless, it is not unusual for women to write about sexual matters: extra-marital affairs, sexual problems with their partners, prostitution or sexual abuse. Over the course of the 25 years I have worked with incarcerated women, fewer than 10 have written or said, "I have a sex addiction." Those who revealed it were incested as children.

PROSTITUTION TO PAY FOR COLLEGE: Costs of college education have peaked over the past several years. This is not a problem for wealthy families. However, young adult children of medium and low-income parents can incur debts of tens of thousands of dollars over a four-year period. The computer makes it easy for them to find Escort Services and "Sugar Daddies" as a way to subsidize their education.

Angora, who was in her 40's when I spoke with her, said her parents told her she was "on my own" after college. The economy was in downfall when she graduated, and she could not find a job. "Prostitution was the only way out that I could see."

Fortunately, she was spared from this indignity when friends allowed her to share space in their apartment.

Donna, a woman of about 25, told me that she seldom bought her own meals while in college. "I date a variety of men. They take me to dinner, and I have leftovers for lunch the next day." In retrospect, I suspect that she was employed as a Call Girl.

Whatever one thinks about women who prostitute, it is hard to deny the hypocrisy of our beliefs about them and our actions toward them.

- Prostitution involves two people, often one a male and the other a female, but most negative societal comment about prostitution involves only the female.

We see a scantily clad Jane Doe soliciting sex, while standing on a street corner in a raunchy U.S. neighborhood. We label her a whore and arrest her. We view a film of a scantily clad woman soliciting sex while seated at a bar in a high-class hotel, label her a star and honor her with an Oscar.

This is not to affirm or deny prostitution as a legitimate sex industry. It is intended to shine light on differing attitudes toward prostitution, offer reasons why women engage in it, and help us identify our own views about prostitution. We need to question why we see prostitution as what the starlet does and reward her, while seeing Jane Doe's prostitution as who she is and condemn her.

Perhaps the stories that follow, as well as those in previous chapters, will help us view the humanity of women who prostitute.

CHAPTER TWENTY:
TRUDY

ALL ROADS LEAD TO PROSTITUTION

*P*olice and the general public see a vastly different version of each prostituting woman than I see. Law enforcement officers may see a woman high on drugs or in the process of breaking a law. She may be verbally or physically combative.

I, on the other hand, meet the women in jail, drug-free, shampooed and intensely ashamed of themselves. I am privy to information about the women's childhood and teenaged years which they write or verbalize to me, as they try to work through their past and create a healthy future.

Trudy was almost 40 when I met her. The story that follows is the Trudy I came to know.

IN TRUDY'S WORDS

"I was born in 1965 in St. Louis City Hospital. My mother told me that she delivered me at 6:20 a.m. and left the hospital with me that evening. Mom said, "you have been in a hurry ever since you were born." Mom was 17 years old, and I was her second child.

"I don't remember much about my dad during my early hears. He was in prison for burglary. I remember grandma, his mother, taking us to what I thought were picnics, only they were visits to prison. I don't remember why or what I thought about him being there. I only remember that we saw him from time to time. He died when I was about 13.

"Mom raised us (me, my younger sister and, later, twin half-brothers) with the help of her parents. We lived downstairs south in a four-family flat, and mom's parents and sisters lived downstairs north. The building had a big yard.

"I remember grandpa being drunk and fighting with my Aunt Pauline – mom's younger sister. Nevertheless, I adored my grandpa. He called me Windy because I was always on the go and talked loudly at about 55 miles an hour. He taught me how to tie my shoes, ride a bike and always bought me a brand-new pair of roller skates for my birthday. He got them for Cathy too. She's a year younger than I am.

"Momma cried a lot and seemed more sad than happy. I thought I caused her unhappiness, but later, after I got older, I thought that she had the same disease of depression that grandma had.

"Grandma's sister, my Great Aunt Charlotte, got momma a job at Southwestern Bell. Momma worked a lot and was always gone.

"When I was four, I remember momma crying in a chair in front of grandma and grandpa. When I asked, they told me momma was going to have two babies. It never occurred to me that my daddy was not around. Not until almost 10 years later would Joe stand there, having beaten up my mother because she took Cathy and me to our dad's funeral, and drunkenly inform us that our twin brothers were his, not our father's.

"Anyhow, in 1970 mother brought home twin baby boys and oh, how I loved them. They looked just alike and were so cute and funny. They would jump in their beds, holding out their hands to each other. Then they'd pull their cribs together and climb in together. Sometimes, we'd get confused about which one was which. We had to remove their diapers because Bernie had a birthmark on his little tush.

"Cathy and I would push their double stroller up and down the sidewalk. Everyone would stop to talk to us. We had our own real baby dolls to play with.

"We went to St. Elsa's Nursery Daycare and I loved it. I loved the nuns and they taught me so much. They took us to the Recreation Center across the street from the downtown projects where we learned to swim.

"Somehow, I knew that momma must have a lot to do at work because she couldn't manage much at home. She gave grandma food stamps and grandma planned and prepared our meals. Manners were a 'must' around grandma and momma often said, 'don't you ever let your grandma hear you say that' whenever we'd say a naughty word or do something impolite.

"Grandma was beautiful, but aloof. To this day my heart goes out to her, but I can't feel hers. 'Mechanical' comes to my mind when I think of this beautiful southern belle. I remember grandpa saying he stepped into some little feed store in Arkansas and saw the prettiest lady in Arkansas. So, he married her. She's close to 75 now.

"Anyhow grandma was never to be told anything that would upset her. And I wasn't supposed to talk too loud. When we'd want a hug, she'd always turn her head for us to kiss her cheek, but she seemed scared when we got close to her. Momma told us later that grandma had shock treatments a long time ago. Momma said she came home from school one day and grandma was in the corner of a room and wouldn't come out and wouldn't let them turn on the lights. Momma said they took grandma away for a while. Ever since, they were told not to upset her.

"I have very fond memories of being a child except that momma cried a lot. I used to always wish I could make her happy. But she often would say things like, 'you kids...' so I thought we were a burden, and we caused her unhappiness.

"It seems like I, more often than not, get on people's nerves. That is something else mom said a lot about me. So, often I was pushed aside to draw my own conclusions about things.

"I've learned now, though, that I wasn't the cause of momma's unhappiness any more than I was the cause of grandma's problems.

"Everybody in my family thought my Uncle Jason was 'it.' He'd come by and fix things or check on us. He'd bring stuff over for Cathy and me. The twins were only about one or two years old at the time and they'd be with the baby-sitter down the street. Cathy got to stay home because she was the quiet one. Uncle Jason would come and take me to the house where he and Aunt Mary lived. My cousin, Sheila, was their only child and she had really neat expensive toys.

"When Aunt Mary was gone, Uncle Jason would take off his clothes and walk around naked, talking and playing with us. This began when I was about four. It stopped when I was eight or nine because my parents moved to another street.

"I had changed my brothers' diapers, so I knew boys were different from girls, but Uncle Jason's privates were so big they scared me. After he was naked, he would have us take off our clothes and we'd have to play with him, and I didn't like his games. He said things we weren't supposed to say and called parts of our bodies names no one else told us. He would put our hands on his privates and stick it in his mouth. Then he would put his mouth down between my legs and ask me how I felt. He'd smile and say, 'you feel it, don't you, you nasty little girl.'

"There it is — a core belief that I've been nasty from that day on."

"Momma had a sister, Patrice, who was eight years older than I was. She used to baby sit Cathy and me. When Patrice was 12 and I was four, Patrice had her friends over for parties. They gave me and Cathy beer and laughed when we got wobbly and fell down.

"I was in Over-Achievers at age 10. My Iowa Test Scores were high in every area and I was selected to attend a school for bright students. Momma was unhappy to have to go to the award ceremony after having worked all day. Grandpa said 'no' to the school because it was downtown in a black neighborhood. 'I don't want you to be around those n-----s,' he said. So, I didn't get to go.

"When I was 10, I got caught up in a child molestation situation. A man promised us money if my friends and I would come to his apartment. He showed us pornographic films, took nude pictures of us, and committed cunnilingus with us. He told us that, if we swallowed his semen, our breasts would grow large, and the boys would really be attracted to us.

"He never paid us, so one day we went to his apartment to collect. He didn't answer the doorbell, so we kept knocking and ran up and down the hall knocking on all of the doors. Police came and we explained that the man owed us money. The cop asked, 'What does he owe you money for?'

"Dottie said, 'we do the dishes for him.'

"One of the man's neighbors was there and told the policeman that it wasn't true – that the man's wife washed his dishes.'

"The policeman asked more questions, and I broke down and told him the truth. Police arrested him. Then the cop took me to my mom and told her about it. Mom broke down crying and I said to myself, 'There, I did it again. I hurt mom again.'

"Mom decided to prosecute but, in court, mom started crying again and when the judge asked me what the man did to me, I told him, 'I don't remember.'

"My friend, Coco told the truth. Afterwards everyone told Coco she did a good job, and they were proud of her. They didn't say anything to me, so I knew I had failed again.

"Drugs were always present in our neighborhood. We thought drugs were cool because Aunt Pauline's friends did drugs. Her friends used to beat up the other kids in the neighborhood, so I thought it was cool that her friends liked me and Cathy. They showed us how to do our hair and that was cool too.

"When I was 11 or 12, my dad got out of prison, but soon returned to crime. His picture was in the newspaper when he got caught in a burglary. He was addicted to prescription drugs, and he and his gang sawed a hole in the roof of a drugstore. The smallest person in the group went through the hole into the store and opened the door for dad and his other friends. They took lots of drugs.

"The newspaper reported that, after the burglary, the men got into a car and took off. Police chased them and shots were fired. A bullet grazed my dad's head. We thought it was cool and we collected newspapers and ran around the neighborhood showing them to everyone.

"I started smoking at home at 13. Mom's second husband, John, wanted us to smoke there instead of sneaking around smoking outside. At 14 or 15, we drank at the bar where mom had gotten a job. That was John's idea too. He had us stand outside the back door to drink so police wouldn't see us.

"At 15 I left home to live with my boyfriend, Lukus. He became my drug. By 16 I was pregnant, and mom talked me into having an abortion. At 18 I had a miscarriage.

"I was drunk in the backseat of a car when I was 19 and was accidentally shot in the back. Lukus was in prison, and I was prostituting in the car.

"I had worked for two years at a fast-food restaurant, but it was very hard work and included cleaning the place after closing hours. So, I went to a bar with a false ID. I was good with people, so the owner gave me a job. I liked it because all I had to do was mix drinks, talk to patrons, and wipe water off the bar. At the same time, I worked a year at a strip club in Illinois. I started hanging out with old school friends who were, by that time, heavily into drugs. They introduced me to cocaine to fill the emptiness I felt while Lukus was in prison. By the time Lukus was released from prison, I wanted cocaine more than I wanted him.

"I had a second abortion at age 21 and a third at age 23. At age 27, my baby was born prematurely and lived only six hours. After the funeral, Lukus gave me $400 to take my family to eat at one restaurant while he took his family to another. On the way home after dinner, mom told me the priest was going to seek manslaughter charges against me because I was using drugs during my pregnancy. I was so ashamed that, after I left my family that night, I bought lots of drugs. When my money was gone, I sneaked around and prostituted with some high-dollared dates that some other prostitutes said would like me because I was young and pretty.

"Ever since then I have put myself on a street corner and didn't care what people thought about me – even in my own neighborhood.

"At age 29 I had a son. I named him Jesu because Jesus Christ gave me another chance.

"My mother died when I was 35. I took care of her after she had a stroke. One day she could see that I was craving drugs. She told me to go. When I came back two hours later, I found her dead at the bathroom door. I wasn't there to help her. I failed again.

"I have not been dry and clean (of alcohol and illegal drugs) for many years except when I was incarcerated. I have hepatitis C from sharing drug needles, and gonorrhea which I got from Lukus."

* * * * *

You will remember that chapter one, which focused on trauma and resilience, reported research that children who experienced four or more adverse childhood experiences (ACE's) had a strong possibility of falling into health and behavior problems. Consider the traumas in Trudy's life:

- living with the severe depression of her mother and grandmother, and thinking their sadness was her fault,
- "Uncle Jason's" sexual exhibitionism and molestation of Trudy and her sister during the years that Trudy was 4-8, followed by him calling her a "nasty little girl," a description she internalized.
- The neighbor man who molested Trudy with oral sex, pornographic films and the filming of Trudy and her friends when Trudy was 10, followed by her belief that she failed her mother in court.

- Trudy's father in and out of prison.
- Introduced, by her mother's second husband, John, to cigarettes at age 13 and to alcohol between the ages of 14-15.
- Her mother forced her into an abortion when she was 16, and she had a miscarriage at age 18.

And the health and behavioral consequences for Trudy? Working in a strip club, prostituting and addicted to cocaine by age 20. Finally, Hepatitis C and Gonorrhea.

In Court, the judge offered Trudy the choice of entering either drug rehabilitation or the Center for Women in Transition (CWIT). The latter is a re-entry program I co-founded. If Trudy enrolled there she could receive the help she needed. She chose CWIT but, instead of going there following release from jail, she sought drugs.

Police caught her, and a judge sentenced her to seven years in a woman's prison. The judge awarded custody of Jesu, Trudy's son, to one of her twin brothers.

Trudy completed her prison sentence. One can only hope that, while incarcerated, she received opportunities for drug rehabilitation, counseling to overcome her sense of failure and increase her self-esteem, and treatment for her medical illnesses.

I have had no follow-up contact with Trudy since she left jail for prison. However, a check of the MO DOC web site shows that she is no longer under state supervision. That means that, unless she moved out-of-state, she completed her prison sentence as well as any years of parole which a judge may have ordered.

Two final notes about Trudy's decline into prostitution:

First: one has to wonder how Trudy's life trajectory might have changed if, when she was 10, her grandfather's racist views had not kept her out of the "school for bright students" located in a black neighborhood. The grandfather's racism glued Trudy to her white family and her white neighborhood, exposing her to the very horrors from which her grandfather sought to protect her. If nothing else, this was a huge example of the negative effects of racism.

Second: Following the funeral of her baby who died following its premature birth, Trudy learned that the priest planned to file homicide charges against her because she used drugs during her pregnancy. Of that information, Trudy wrote: "I was so ashamed after I left...that night..." that she bought lots of drugs and prostituted, and "ever since then I have put myself on a street corner and didn't care what people thought about me – even in my own neighborhood."

Like Trudy's grandfather, the priest probably acted out of anger, ignorance or his own personality deformities. Certainly, he displayed ignorance of the Christian Gospel's consistent message to align oneself with people on the edges of society and to forgive.

Writing circles teach that each protagonist has "a hole in their soul," which their behaviors attempt to fill. The hole in Trudy's soul seems clear – her belief that she, personally, was defective.

A great chasm exists between the belief that one's <u>work</u> is defective and the belief that one's very <u>self</u> is defective. The hole in Trudy's soul falls in both categories but shows most profoundly in the belief that she was, in her words, "nasty." Condemnation only deepens the hole. What she needed for healing was an abundance of love – unconditional love.

Resilience studies show that a single person (teacher, grandparent, neighbor, etc.) who takes a sincere interest in a traumatized child can change her life for the better. That fact reiterates the oft-quoted anonymous saying that:

"To the world, you are only a single person but to one person, you may be the world."

One has to wonder if, in the "school for bright students," Trudy might have found or been singled out by that one person who saw her internal goodness and helped her nurture it? What a shame that she did not have that opportunity.

CHAPTER TWENTY-ONE:
KAYE

DISSOCIATIVE AMNESIA: BECOMING A "MADAM"

*K*aye is the third of four children. One brother, seven years older than she, died in a fire. A second sibling, five years older than Kaye, moved to another city (no reason given). Her only sister, one year younger than Kaye, was also, according to Kaye, molested as a child.

IN KAYE'S WORDS

"I come from a loving family. I am the third child. I had two older brothers and a younger sister. Although I'm not the youngest, I've been treated as the baby of the family. I had a happy sheltered and privileged childhood.

"Most of our activities (TV, radio, curfew and bedtime) were monitored. We couldn't go to friends' homes until mom first met or phoned their parents. Mom was very strict, and I remember telling myself that, when I got older and had a child, I would not be so strict. But it's true what they say: you turn into your parents when you have your own children. I was just as strict with my child and, maybe, even stricter than mom.

"We grew up in the suburbs with the best of everything. Yet we never looked down on anyone or thought that we were better than those that didn't have what we had. In fact, we were taught to share with those less fortunate than we were and to give our best – not the things we didn't want anymore. And we earned most of what we got. We were not brats.

"Although I wasn't the youngest, I was daddy's little girl. I could do no wrong in his eyes. I was the happiest little girl in the world until my daddy died when I was eight years old. I still lived a privileged life after he died, but his death left a huge void in me. I still wonder today how my life would have been if he were still here.

"After dad died, mom dated another guy. He almost raped me when I was nine, but mom came home and found him undressing me. She ran him out of the house, and never brought any men friends to the house after that.

"I ran away from home for the first time (the first time I can remember) when I was 12 years old. I used to stay gone for days at a time. I didn't know, at the time, why I ran away. I wasn't a rebellious child. I made very good grades in school. I gave no one any reason to think I would run away and yet, suddenly I would disappear. I did this three-to-five times a year. If you had asked me why I did it, I would tell you I didn't know because I didn't know.

"Usually, I went to a friend's home when I ran away. Once I went to a home-less shelter, but they called my mother, and she came and took me home.

"Years later, in drug rehab, I realized that from age three to 11, I was sex-ually abused by various male relatives. I had blocked it out totally. I would simply run away because I didn't trust my relatives. I didn't know it then, but I later realized that, when they were around, I felt threatened by them. I learned, during those runaway times, how to survive on the streets and some of those habits, like prostitution, I hung onto as an adult. That's how I ended up in jail.

"I married my first husband when I was 19. He was very handsome but totally abusive. When I was 24, I told him to leave, and I moved to Iowa to get away from him. I was o.k. there for six weeks.

"Then I moved to Omaha where I met my second husband, a man from West Africa. He was not abusive at all. I promised him that I would not smoke crack or sabotage our relationship.

In the second year of our marriage, he joined the Marines and was in Oklahoma, so I moved to Oklahoma. I loved him but I was not "in love" with him.

"When he was transferred to North Carolina, I came to St. Louis. We are still married but have been separated for three years because he cheated on me. I don't know where he is today.

"To support myself, I had an escort service and ran ads in the black newspaper. Police, in a sting operation, phoned my agency. I did not have anyone available to go out on the call, so I went myself. The police didn't arrest me for prostitution, but I had a Tylenol #3 (Tylenol with Codeine) in my purse, and they charged me with Class C felony drug possession. (Apparently, a judge sentenced her to probation, not prison).

"A few months later police picked me up for speeding. Because I had a felony on my record, the judge sentenced me to Choices, the drug rehab program at the County Jail. I completed Choices and was released with three-years-probation.

"After my release from jail, I lived on the streets. I didn't report to my probation officer because I figured she'd send me back to jail when she learned I was homeless.

But fifteen months later I turned myself in, and I am currently incarcerated.

"I started getting high on marijuana at 16 years old. To cover up the pain that I couldn't explain.

I started snorting cocaine at about 20 years old and I began smoking crack cocaine when I was 26.

"I've had a few years of clean time (without drugs) in my adult years and have had periods of sobriety (from alcohol), but at one point or another I would eventually return to what felt good or comfortable to me.

"I've been in drug treatment 12 times over these many years. These included St Louis County's Choices Program which I mentioned previously. In Oklahoma, when I was 30, I only stayed in treatment for 10 days. In North

Carolina I completed three weeks in a rehab unit. At age 33, I detoxed for three days each, in three different hospitals: East St. Louis MO, Granite City MO and Belleville IL. At age 35, I left [treatment] after four or five weeks in a hospital in Caseyville, MO. Then I completed 91 days in that same hospital. It was during this last stay in the Caseyville Center that I remembered my childhood sexual abuse.

"Lately I have been working through the pain without drugs. While I've been locked up this time, I've learned to love myself, feel the pain and not cover it up. I think I'm almost ready to start helping others who have been through – or who are going through – what I have experienced."

* * * * *

In session #7 of *Becoming All We Can Be*, my course at the Buzz Westfall Justice Center, the women students focus on their giftedness. Prior to discussing the eight kinds of intelligence, we look at activities which they enjoyed as children and teens. Occasionally a woman will write, in her homework, that she cannot remember much of her early life. Sometimes she goes on to say, as did Kaye, that she did not remember that she had been incested until much later when she was in therapy.

As a point of interest, she noted in class #7, that she has a talent for photography. She likes every aspect of it. "I become the camera" she said. She was so energized by this conversation that I suspect she is now a photographer.

The most recent (2013) edition of the Psychiatric Association's *Diagnostic and Statistical Manual* of Mental Disorders includes dissociative amnesia under the category of Dissociative Disorders. "The main symptom is memory loss that's more severe than normal forgetfulness and that can't be explained by a medical condition. A 'dissociate' can't recall information about herself or events and people in her life, especially from a traumatic time. Dissociative amnesia can be specific to events in a certain time...It may sometimes involve travel or confused wandering away from your life (dissociative fugue). An episode usually occurs suddenly and may last...years".

Regarding dissociative fugue, you will recall that Kaye ran away or disappeared for periods of time during her childhood.

The inner work that Kaye did in her last session in drug rehab and her participation in Becoming All We Can Be apparently healed the traumas of her childhood. She has had no additional arrests for drug possession or prostitution. My hope is that she has established herself in society as a great photographer.

CHAPTER TWENTY-TWO: RICKIE

TRAFFICKED BY HER MOTHER

Rickie's parents, Alena and Allen, were 27 and 40 respectively when Rickie was born. Rickie was her mother's sixth child. Allen also fathered Alena's fifth and seventh children, Korey and Celena, but not the other five.

Rickie's parents separated when she was five. Rickie has seen her father only three or four times since her parents' separation. However, she knows where he lives and, before being imprisoned, phoned him about twice a year.

Trafficking of women receives a lot of media coverage these days. In most instances, the crime results when strangers lure runaways, other teens and women, with promises of lucrative careers. The stranger, a "pimp," makes prostitutes or domestic servants of the women.

IN RICKIE'S WORDS

"My mother's first child was born when she was 19. She had seven children by the time she was 28 and an eighth at age 35. She died in 2002 at age 55, from complications of gall bladder surgery. I was 28 at the time of her death. My father is still living.

"My father wanted my mother to stay home with us kids, but she wanted to party. I remember the day my mother left my father. It was a big fight – blood everywhere. Glass and things all over the house. I was five. My mother took us to our grandmother's house and left.

"My grandmother was hard as nails. She called me names that nobody should be called: monkey, little nigger, black-assed little girl, and ugly.

"Celena, a year younger than me, was light-skinned, so grandma liked her a whole lot better than she liked me. I could walk by our grandmother, and she would hit me because I didn't walk fast enough. I would pick up my pace and she would hit me for walking too fast.

"I remember being seven and having Christmas at my Auntie's house. I got this baby doll that had a stroller and walked on her tippy toes as she pushed the stroller. She was the sweetest little doll ever.

"When Christmas break was over, we went back to grandma's house. I played with my baby doll whenever I had time, but I didn't have a lot of time. Grandma kept me busy with chores. One day, grandma picked up my baby doll, tore off her head and threw her into the furnace. Then she pitched my doll's body into the furnace too. I cried and cried for days and asked, 'Why did you do that?' She told me I looked too happy and she wanted to wipe the happy off my face. I couldn't stand her after that. I stopped smiling for a long time.

"My grandad was sick, so grandma put him in a nursing home a couple blocks down the street. I would go visit him two or three times a week. Grandma never went to visit him after she made sure my sister, Celena, and I were visiting him.

"When I was eight, grandma would have a man come over. I'd be in the room and she'd have me lay under the bed. She put on dirty movies, the XXX rated ones. When I think back, it could have been to throw me off, so I would think the sounds were coming from the TV instead of from her and that man. I didn't know anything about sex at that time.

"Sometimes my auntie would let us visit her. She was real nice but my cousin would wake me out of my sleep, get on top of me and pump up and down. My oldest brother did it too. They took turns.

"Sometimes my auntie's boyfriend sent her to the store, and he would have me rub his privates and put his private parts on top of mine and rub until he got off. He was very nasty, and he smelled like booze and stuff all the time.

"I was almost ten when my mother got her own place and moved six of us kids in with her. My oldest brother stayed with my auntie. It was nice for a while but then my mother started leaving again.

"After she was gone, my brothers, Richard and Korey, who were one and three years older than I, would rummage through garbage and steal food for us. Or they'd go to the park and bring home fish and snails that we'd boil and eat. We always went to school so we could have breakfast.

"The kids in school teased me all the time. I had to wear Priscilla's clothes and they didn't fit because she was shorter than me. The kids called me 'black and dirty and ugly.' They called me 'bald-headed' too. The teacher would laugh when they said this stuff. I sat in class not learning anything. The teachers passed me to the next grade just for coming to class.

"My first-grade teacher pushed my head into the classroom door and chipped my two front teeth. He was the first man to hit me. I was seven when this happened. Because of this, I lost a front tooth and my teeth rotted. I have low self-confidence because of my looks. It pisses me off more than anything I've been through in life.

"I met this girl in sixth grade. She wasn't in any of my classes, but she heard the kids make fun of me. One day as I walked home from school, she pulled me to the side and told me she had some clothes she'd give me. She took me to her house and gave me two pairs of pants and four shirts. I said, 'thank you.'

"She wouldn't talk to me at school but, if she saw me away from school, she would speak to me. Once I said 'hi' to her when she was with her friends.

She got mad and wouldn't speak to me after that. I felt so sick on the inside because I ran off the only nice person I knew. I went home and cried.

"Sometimes my mother would come by and stay a few days. Then she'd be gone again. I became resentful toward her and told her I wished I lived with my father. She came at me with a knife, and I ran out of the house. I went to my auntie's house and told her what happened. Auntie told me to go back home so I did. My mother didn't say much to me after that.

"My brother and me were put out of the apartment because we couldn't pay the rent. My other aunt told us about an apartment next door to her, so we moved there. It was run by a slum lord. When things broke, they stayed broke. Nothing ever got fixed. My uncle raped me in that apartment when I was 12 ½.

"I was 13 and walking home from school one day when I heard someone call my name. As I got closer, I saw it was my mother. She was sitting in a car with some man. She told me to get in, so I got in the back seat. She said 'This is Jeffrey, and he likes you. I want you to spend some time with him.' She got out of the car and told me to get up front, but I didn't. She closed the door and walked away. Then, with me still in the back seat, he drove off and took me to live with him.

'Jeffrey and I lived on the second floor of a house. His mother lived on the first floor. She was a nice lady. She taught me how to eat proper like. And she bought me clothes and showed me how to dress, and how to stand with my head up like I was a somebody.

"I graduated from eighth grade and registered for high school before I went to Jeffrey's house. But he didn't want me to go back to school. He said he had enough education for the both of us.

"I've never told anyone what I'm about to write. When I was sixteen, I got pregnant with Jeffrey's baby. I was playing with Jeffrey's little nephew, and I fell down some stairs. I remember having a lot of pain that night. I went to the bathroom and blood and the baby came out. It looked like a bunch of veins. I was scared and didn't know what to do. I just dropped it in the toilet and flushed. Since I've now had kids of my own, I know I had to be at least eight to ten weeks pregnant at the time. I still think about it. I never told Jeffrey.

"As the years went by, I saw my mother – maybe three times. Sometimes, when Jeffrey would drive us into the neighborhood, I'd see other family members too.

"Jeffrey never was abusive to me until the day I said I wanted to leave. I had heard his niece say she was going to college and make something of herself. After that I started thinking about my own future and the things I wanted to do. I talked to Jeffrey about it. He told me no way would I be able to do those things because I'd never been to high school.

"Later, we were over to his sister's house, and I saw one of my cousins walking down the street. She told me about this place called Job Corps and said they could help me with my dreams. But she didn't know the phone number. Two months later I saw a TV commercial about the Job Corps, and I wrote down the number. At about the same time, I learned that Jeffrey got his girlfriend pregnant.

"I told him I was leaving. He got real mad and hit me in the nose. My nose started to bleed. He cried and told me how sorry he was for hurting me. He said he didn't want me to leave him. After that, whenever he would leave for work, he would lock me in, making it impossible for me to go anywhere until he got home.

"I decided to be real nice to him so he would think I wanted to stay. After some time passed, he took the locks off the doors, and I would leave the house after he went to work. While I was out one day, I met this man who liked me. I was 19. I don't know exactly how old he was, but he was older than Jeffrey. We went on a date.

"I didn't know it at the time, but Jeffrey had told his niece to watch me. When I got home, Jeffrey slapped me, punched me in the stomach and cut off my hair. Then he cut off my clothes and made me get into a tub of hot water. He scrubbed my body hard and cursed me. He said I was a stupid, cheating whore. Then he got me out of the tub, raped me and said, 'I'm gonna make sure you never f___ another man again. He took my under clothes, put them on a serving tray and set them on fire.

"When he turned back to the fire, I ran out of the house, naked and screaming. I ran down the street, but nobody was around. Then a man came out of a house and yelled, 'Watch out. He's got a bat.'

"I ducked down because he was swinging the bat toward my head. I took off running again but Jeffrey caught me before I got to the end of the block. He grabbed my arm and said 'just come home and get some clothes. I'll let you go but come and put on some clothes first.' I started to go back with him because I was so scared the way he was holding my arm.

"This one lady saw this and didn't believe Jeffrey. She followed us back to the house and said, 'I'm going to call the police.' She asked if I was afraid of him, and I said 'yes.' She told him I was leaving with her, and she was going to phone the police.

"Jeffrey said, 'you don't have to. She can go if that's what she wants.'

"So, I went with her and called my cousin, Alice. She (Alice) told me how to get to my auntie's house and that's where I went. My auntie hadn't seen me in a long time and said I could stay.

"Jeffrey paid my cousin to tell him where I was, and he found me two days later. He tried to get me to go home with him by bringing some of my clothes to me. He came to auntie's house a few times and we would do a clothes exchange. He'd give me some of my clothes from his house but, first, he'd make me give him the clothes I already had. We did this clothes exchange for a couple of months before he finally realized I wasn't going back with him."

I encourage women in my course to write about their pain. This is a poem Rickie wrote.

"BROKEN

Pieces everywhere.
Big, little, every size.
Long broken pieces.
Where is the glue?
Where should I start?
From the outside in or the inside out?
I'll just start and see.
With the pain so strong, so true, so blue,
Will I be able to put the pieces
Back together again?
I wonder.
I'm so broken…"

Rickie continues her story:

"I lived at auntie's house for about five months. Then she started asking me for money. I prostituted to pay her.

"Then I saw the Job Corps commercial again and wrote down the number. I phoned and got an appointment to meet them. Two weeks later I was in job training in Indiana. I was shocked that so many people were there. The classes were hard for me, but I was good in the trade I chose – Cement Mason. I liked it a lot and learned how to mix cement, set forms, and pour concrete around the center of different projects.

"Nine months into the program, when I was twenty, I got real sick. I threw up everything I ate. I even threw up the water. Job Corps made me take a medical leave. I went to Chicago to be with my oldest sister, Priscilla, who needed a baby-sitter. I hadn't seen her in five years and was glad I could help out.

"Priscilla told me a lot of things that went on with my mother and father and about how my father (who was not her birth father) sexually abused her.

"I asked, 'Is that why my mother left him?'

"She said, 'No. He would say to our mother 'If you don't spend any time with me, I guess I will be with your daughter. And she left anyway and that's what he did.'

"I was sick to my stomach when she told me this. I had always longed for my father to be in my life, and this information broke my heart. But, crazy as it seems, instead of being angry with him, I started to dislike Priscilla.

"Priscilla called another auntie and told her about me. Auntie lived in Alabama and invited me to come visit her for the summer. She had gotten married, had a baby, and seemed very happy. I wanted what she had so I spent the summer with her. While there I attended the funeral of my brother-in-law's aunt and ended up meeting Amos. We talked on the phone every night and he came to see me a few times. Then I went to live with him.

"That was a big mistake. He beat me so bad that I couldn't open my mouth. After that I tried killing myself. He had a lot of pills in the cabinet, and I swallowed about 90 of them. He came home just in time to rush me to the hospital. They pumped my stomach. When I woke up, I asked why they saved me. I just wanted to die.

"Amos took me back to his house and, when we got there, he jumped on me and raped me. I was living a nightmare all over again. I ran out of the house and ended up breaking a neighbor's window. It was about 2:00 a.m. and very dark. The man of the house came out and I ran inside with his wife. My arm was bleeding and blood was dripping all over the floor. This lady gave me a robe and took care of me. Amos came inside and said this was our business and the neighbors should let me go back with him.

"The woman told Amos she was calling the police and that I wasn't going anywhere with him. I was very thankful. These neighbors took me to the hospital where I got stitches. They got me a hotel room for the night, and the next morning put me on a bus to Chicago.

"When I got to Chicago, I went back to my auntie's house – the auntie where I had to prostitute in order to stay with her.

I called Darryl, a man I had previously spoken to as a friend. We developed a wonderful relationship that was fun. I was arm candy for him. I had been living with him for about a year when he asked me to marry him. We never set a date, but we did say our vows before God to be with each other.

"Eventually I went back to Job Corps. My trade this time was Apartment Maintenance. I really enjoyed it. I stayed there for ten months, coming home on weekends to be with my husband.

"Two weeks before my 23rd birthday, I learned that I was pregnant. Darryl and I both wanted the pregnancy, but it prevented me from continuing in my trade, so I began Nurse Aide Classes.

"Having my son was overwhelming for me. When I was in the hospital, I felt something strange. I asked the nurse, 'What is that?'

"She looked at me strange-like and asked, 'What are you talking about?'

"I told her something was pounding in my chest. She said that it was my heart beating – that I was in love with my baby. I looked down on my son and smiled. I knew then what it was to love. I wanted to protect him from everything and everyone.

"Darryl and I lived together for seven years. He taught me to read so I could read to our son. However, I wasn't able to lose the weight I gained when I was pregnant. I just gained more and more, and I couldn't lose that either.

"Darryl didn't like me after that. He told me, when I was 27, that he wasn't going to support both me and our son and that I should get out. I prostituted to support myself, but I never did it when my son was visiting me.

"Eventually I met another man, Harold, in an online chat room. I told him my problems and he said, 'Come to Dallas and I'll take care of you.' When I got there, I found out that he was 67, not 50 like he had told me. I was only 34. I stayed with Harold less than four months and was three months pregnant when I left him.

"I phoned Trayon whom I had met several years earlier in St. Louis. He was nice to me even though I was pregnant with another man's baby. We really loved each other. Trayon was good to Ivon, my son, when Ivon came to spend time with us.

"I went into a big depression when my daughter was born, and I could hardly get out of bed for about two months. I didn't want anything to do with my baby when she was born, but Trayon took care of her 'til I was better.

"Then I got pregnant again and the same thing happened. Eventually, I guess, Trayon got tired of me being fat and depressed. He started being mean to me. My son, Ivon asked, 'Why do you let him treat you like that?' and went back to stay with Darryl, his father.

"I took the girls and went to a shelter for abused women but, after we had been there for three months, the building was turned into a shelter for tornado victims. (A tornado decimated the town of Joplin MO in May, 2011 and sent victims to various cities, like St. Louis, for shelter). We didn't have any other place to go so I took my little girls and went back to Trayon.

"When I was pregnant with my fourth child, I learned that Trayon was seeing other women. He got mad when I confronted him about it, put his hands around my neck and tried to choke me. When I couldn't breathe, he released his grip and left the house. I was afraid he would finish the job when he came back so I got his gun from a drawer to protect myself.

"He grabbed the gun from me when he got back. It went off and a bullet shot through his shoulder. I dialed 911. The ambulance took Trayon to the hospital. Police took my little girls, not quite two and three years old, to the Department of Family Services (DFS), and they brought me to jail."

* * * * *

I labelled Rickie's case as trafficking in concert with the United States' Trafficking Victims Protection Act (TVPA). Part A of the act reads: [Trafficking is] "a commercial sex act, induced by force, fraud or coercion, or in which the person induced to perform such act has not attained 18 years of age... Part B of the act reads: [Trafficking is] "obtaining a person for labor or service... through the use of force, fraud, or coercion for the purpose of subjugation to involuntary servitude..."

Rickie's situation fits both A and B of the Act. The case is unusual in that Rickie's mother – not a stranger - handed her over to Jeffrey.

Rickie spent several months in jail where she gave birth to her fourth child. DFS took the baby from Rickie when Maleina was one day old and returned her and the other two children to Trayon after he recovered from his wounds.

Trayon told Rickie that he did not press charges against her. However, Missouri law considers crimes to be committed against the state, so the state charged her with 'Domestic Assault, 1st degree with serious injury' (the bullet pierced Trayon's shoulder and collapsed a lung), and 'Armed Criminal Action (ACA)'.

While jailed, Rickie enrolled in my course and wrote her story which you have just read. Because her financial status did not allow her to hire a private attorney, the state assigned a public defender (PD) to her. The PD seldom visited her and was replaced, two months before her sentencing, by a second PD. (The first PD died a few months later. I suspect that she (the PD) was seriously ill at the time she was attempting to defend Rickie.)

The jail psychologist suggested to Rickie that her case should be prosecuted as a domestic violence case. However, the prosecutor refused this idea.

Rickie consistently denied having any intention of shooting Trayon. Her intention was simply to defend herself from him. Although she occasionally smoked marijuana, she had no drug addictions and no prior arrests.

Nevertheless, the prosecutor insisted on charging her. He offered two options: 1. Take the case to trial and he would make certain that Rickie would spend 24 years in prison. (This, of course, was an empty threat because a jury, not the prosecutor, would decide her guilt or innocence. However, Rickie did not know this and, apparently, her PD did not explain it to her).

2. Plead guilty ('Domestic Assault, 1st Degree with serious injury' and 'Armed Criminal Action') and he would recommend that Rickie's sentence be reduced to 12 years in prison.

Through her 14 months in jail, Rickie insisted she had not intended to hurt Trayon. However, fearing that she would never see her children again, Rickie pleaded guilty and, at the time (January, 2022), is still in prison.

In the meantime, Trayon divorced her and has custody of the three youngest children. In the early years of her imprisonment, Trayon allowed Rickie to phone his residence to speak to the children. However, in the past several years, he has not accepted her calls. To be fair to Trayon, calls from prison to families are expensive.

Before her trial, while she participated in my course in the Buzz Westfall Justice Center, I encouraged Rickie to write about the pain within her.

This poem is named FREEDOM.

"FREEDOM

Get it out!
Get it Out!
I cry to myself, you won't break, just
Get it Out! Get it Out!
For goodness sake,
You'll be fine. You will see.
By holding on to it, you can't be
The Person you were meant to be, so
Get it Out!
Your mind is trapped like an animal in a cage
And you're so full of rage.
If you have to scream and shout,
Do it.
Just get it out
Before it's too late.
My soul is crying out, set me free.
So I can be the person I was meant to be."

Only designated amounts of clothing and other items can be taken from the Buzz Westfall Justice Center to prison when a person is transferred from the one institution to another. Rickie's books of poems could not be taken. Jail officers told her that they would hold those books of poems for a few days until someone claimed them for her. Unfortunately, she had no one to claim them for her and, as a result, she has lost those poems.

In the early months of her imprisonment, I mailed Rickie, through Barnes & Noble's warehouse, a few paperback journals so she could continue writing her poems. However, during the past two years, although those journals were totally paper as required (no cardboard or hardbacks) and were sent directly from the Barnes and Noble warehouse, CO's at the prison refused to give them to her.

Rickie hopes that the Parole Board will hear her case and release her for good behavior.

In late 2018, I wrote two letters to the man who was, at that time, Prosecuting Attorney. In it I outlined what I saw as the injustices in Rickie's case. I asked for an appointment to speak to him about her situation. He did not respond to either letter.

Rickie is scheduled to appear before the Parole Board on August 25, 2022.

I have made plans for her to come to St. Louis's Center for Women in Transition where she will receive the help she needs until she is ready to live on her own. It is possible, and even probable that, with CWIT's help, Rickie will eventually be able to re-connect with her children.

CHAPTER TWENTY-THREE: PROBLEMS FOR WOMEN IN THE STATE JUSTICE SYSTEM

*H*aving learned the childhood/teen problems that catapulted women into drugs, prostitution, crime and jail, it is now time to name the indignities they suffer DURING incarceration. Many problems are experienced by both imprisoned women and men. These include inadequate nutrition; lack of access to dental care; insufficient toilet paper; chaos and confusion created for inmates when officers interpret and execute rules differently; night noise and lights that interfere with deep sleep; lack of privacy created by the presence of toilets in shared cells; inadequate educational opportunities; distances between hometowns and correctional facilities; environmental problems such as limited access to fresh air and the relative absence of live greenery to absorb pollutants and add oxygen to the air.

Justice-involved-women, simply because they are women, experience problems not faced by men. Some of these are:

1. rules against physical touch;

2. limited visits from children. (Mothers ordinarily take their children to visit their imprisoned fathers, but the reverse occurs much less frequently);

3. Sexual assaults by corrections officers. (Male prisoners are often assaulted by other male prisoners. Women are most frequently assaulted by carceral officers.);

4. Pregnancy, Labor, Delivery, and Care of Newborns;

5. Release from imprisonment during night hours.

We will consider each of these concerns separately.

1. RULES AGAINST PHYSICAL TOUCH.

Physical touch is a natural gesture for many women. We embrace in solidarity when we cry and when we laugh. We extend a hand to strangers and hug friends. We place an arm around a shoulder to signal support.

In many carceral facilities, touching is a punishable act. Fear undergirds the "no touching" rule:

- fear of spreading scabies, lice, and infectious diseases,
- fear that touch will escalate into violence. This is more likely for males than females, but jail and prison rules tend to be "one size fits all," and
- fear that touch might escalate into genital activity.

Do these problems occur in penal institutions? Of course – just as they occur in schools and dormitories where youth and young adults live in close proximity. However, school principals do not curb the problem by creating "no touch" rules.

No-touch rules deprive justice-involved-women of the healing benefits of touch.

Bessel A. van der Kolk, M.D., in the foreword to Psychologist/Author Peter A. Levine's book, *Trauma and Memory* wrote that [we need to] "understand the enormous power of touch to help people borrow comfort and physiological safety from each other."

(Peter A. Levine. *Trauma and Memory: Brain and Body in a Search for the Living Past*. Berkeley, CA: North Atlantic Books. 1997).

Recently a woman in my course in the jail cried as she vented her frustrations with her lawyer. "I need a hug," she said, so another incarcerated woman and I held her until her sobbing subsided. But, in doing so, we subjected her and the other woman to possible "lock-down" (solitary confinement) and put my teaching position in jeopardy. Depriving a woman of human touch lessens her opportunities to heal the traumas that propelled her into law-breaking activity in the first place.

2. LIMITED VISITS FROM CHILDREN.

Although the majority of crimes occur in heavily populated cities, federal and state governments build most prisons in small towns and rural areas. The women's prison closest to St. Louis is in Vandalia Missouri, two hours travel time in light traffic. A distance of 1 ½ hours separates Omaha children from their mothers in a Lincoln NE prison. Miami children live 4 ½ hours from their mothers in the Hernando Corrections Center in Brookville, FL.

At times, family members arrive for a pre-arranged visit only to be told that the women are "locked down" and cannot receive visitors. Caregivers then have to attend to the visiting children's grief.

Betsy, a woman in jail told me officers turned away her mother, a large woman with asthma and arthritis when, in the heat of summer, her mother arrived at the jail in a sleeveless dress. (Jail rules require "appropriate clothing" but officers and visitors may have differing interpretations of the word "appropriate").

I observed an officer turning away Judy's mother and three pre-school aged children, including a baby in her arms. Visiting rules allowed only two children per adult visitor.

In St. Louis County's 1200 inmate Buzz Westfall Justice Center, mothers are not allowed to hold their children, although the facility is a jail and not a prison. All visits, no matter the child's age or the mother's charges, take place in telephone styled booths with a glass panel separating the mother from her visitors. "Guilty until proven innocent" seemed to be the facility's policy.

3. SEXUAL ASSAULTS BY OFFICERS.

On September 4, 2003, President George W. Bush signed into law a national Prison Rape Elimination Act (PREA). The bill established a commission to draft standards intended to eliminate prison sexual assault.

However, sexual assault continues to occur in jails and prisons.

At the end of a workday in the County Jail Laundry, the supervising CO offered Marilee a cigarette. (Smoking is against jail rules.) She gladly smoked one with him, after which he told her that she owed him.

Catch 22!

If she refused, he could report her for smoking. If she reported that he forced her into sex with him, he could deny it, and report her for smoking. PREA does not provide protection against retaliation for reporting sexual assaults.

This incident occurred about 10 years ago. Today, jails and prisons post signs encouraging inmates to report sexual misconduct. The problem may be reduced but it is far from eliminated.

Readers may conclude that these are isolated cases. They are not.

> According to the Bureau of Justice Statistics, around 80,000 women and men a year are sexually abused in America's correctional facilities. That number is almost certainly subject to underreporting, through shame or a victim's fear of retaliation.

> (Bureau of Justice Statistics reported in Chandra Bozelko, *"Why We Let Prison Rape Go On*: The New York Times. April 17, 2015).

4. PREGNANCY, LABOR, DELIVERY, CARE of NEWBORN BABIES.

Incarceration holds some benefits for pregnant women. It provides shelter for the homeless, regularly timed meals, and a drug-free environment for drug-addicted women. It offers the possibility of pre-natal care for women who lacked access to that service, and it protects women and their unborn babies from spousal/partner abuse.

The Eighth Amendment requires carceral facilities to offer prenatal care to expectant mothers, but the quantity and quality of that care varies between institutions.

In the facility where I taught, pregnant women received double portions of all food. That translated into four slices of bread per meal and two portions of a cake dessert for both the noon and evening meals. Obviously, ingesting that load of carbohydrates adds more pounds than is healthy for either pregnant women or their unborn babies.

To avoid the possibility of jailed women making cheap wine out of fresh fruit, many carceral facilities refuse to serve fresh fruit to prisoners. Pregnant women are not exempted from this rule. They receive no fresh fruits, but they do receive milk, daily Calcium and Vitamin D tablets.

5. RELEASE FROM JAIL DURING NIGHT HOURS.

Jail officers release many women between midnight and 6:00 a.m. Women in my classes were unsure of the reason but thought their release time matched their arrest time. This caused no problem for women whose family members were able and willing to pick them up in the middle of the night. However, it caused anxiety in others who had to walk alone, in the dark of night, to the bus station two blocks south of the jail.

Alli begged me repeatedly to meet her at 2:00 a.m. at the jail and drive her to the bus which would take her to a safe house in Joplin, MO. She wanted to leave St. Louis because she feared drug dealers who, she thought, would be waiting for her outside the jail. Because of my night blindness, I could not honor her request.

On the day following her release, I phoned the safe house supervisor who had agreed to meet Alli's bus. Alli was not on that bus. Nor did she arrive on the next bus a few hours later.

Apparently, this night release practice is widespread. Journal reports indicate that the practice is required in order to make certain that inmates are released exactly at the time of the day or night in which they were arrested. So if the person is arrested at 2:30 a.m., she must be released at 2:30 a.m.

A July, 2019 issue of Mother Jones reported that a San Francisco Sheriff's Department issues taxi vouchers to men and women released after 8 p.m., and that a D.C. jail makes certain that transportation, housing, and prescription medications are provided to night released justice-involved-women.

What a shame that compassionate acts like those of the San Francisco and D.C. Sheriffs are not available, in other cities, to women released after dark.

A. SHACKLING.

Some jails and prisons shackle women's wrists and ankles to hospital gurneys during labor and delivery, although I found no recorded incident of a women in labor slipping off a cart and escaping from a carceral facility. Some defend the shackling practice as a precaution against the possibility that a laboring woman might injure an attending officer.

The fact that a law exists on the books does not ensure that information about the law trickles down to officers responsible to remove shackles from women in the last trimester of pregnancy.

Shackles and chains during labor and delivery – and even during the third trimester of pregnancy – are impediments to safe care of pregnant women. For this reason, health organizations oppose them.

B. VIOLENCE BY OFFICERS.

Journals have reported that officers have tased women who failed to respond as quickly to orders as the officers demanded. Pregnant women are not exempt from this practice.

C. MISTREATMENT AND RAPE DURING PREGNANCY.

Prison Legal News has reported instances in which pregnant detainees have been raped by officers.

D. NEWBORNS IN JAILS AND PRISONS:

What happens to the babies after they are born? In most instances, mothers are alerted, ahead of their delivery due date to name a family member or friend who can provide "kincare" until the mother's release. Most jails and prisons allow a mother to keep the baby with her for only one to three days.

If the baby's mother is jailed near the caretaker and if she has no drugs or alcohol in her body, some institutions allow her to pump breast milk for the caretaker to feed the baby. If the carceral facility is located at a distance, this is not possible, so the baby is deprived of the antibodies in the mother's milk.

If the mother has no family or friends willing and able to take the infant, the Department of Family Services (DFS) places it in foster care. Some foster parents keep the mother informed, by photos and letters, about the growth and health of the baby. However, not all foster parents do this.

Occasionally, when a child is moved from one foster family to another, an incarcerated mother loses track of her child's whereabouts. Felicia, one of my jailed students, aged out of foster care when she reached 18. She married her boyfriend, Rico, who had for several years been fostered with her, but who had eventually been adopted. Neither of them knew their birth kin so they "familied" with a group of youth who, like themselves, had aged out of foster care with no place to go.

Stealing and prostitution supplemented their minimum wage jobs.

A drive-by shooting killed Rico when Felicia was eight months pregnant. Police work following Rico's death revealed a warrant for Felicia's arrest.

Shortly afterwards, Felicia's baby was born in jail and DFS took her child. Felicia's case worker, tried unsuccessfully, over a period of three weeks, to learn where DFS had placed the baby. Felicia's grief was immense as she mourned the death of her husband and the "disappearance" of her baby.

Eventually the puzzle unraveled. DFS had refused to share the baby's location because, expecting the baby's father to take custody of her, they feared giving the baby's location to anyone else. Inter-agency communication had failed to report Rico's death. The DFS staff became much more cooperative once they learned that Felicia was alone in life.

Sometimes a state severs the relationship of children from their parents.

The Adoption and Safe Families Act (ASFA) was enacted in 1997 in response to concerns that many children were remaining in foster care for long periods or experiencing multiple placements. This landmark legislation requires timely permanency planning for children and emphasizes that the child's safety is of paramount concern. [Among other things, it] requires States to file for termination of parental rights (TPR) once children have been in foster care for 15 of the most recent 22 months, except in certain allowable circumstances, and encourages States to expedite TPR in specific situations of severe harm inflicted on children.

(Child and Family Services Review: Information Portal. "Adoption and Safe Families Act (ASFA) https://www/cfsrportal.acf.hhs.gov 2017).

Eleven U.S. women's prisons sponsor nurseries where a select group of new mothers can bond with their babies and learn parenting skills. John Caniglia, reporter for the Plain Dealer in Cleveland OH, located those nurseries in Cleveland, Poona CA, Newark DE, Decatur IL, Indianapolis IN, Southeast NE, Bedford Hills NY, Marysville OH, Pierre SD, Gig Harbor WA and West Columbia WVA.

Requirements for admission to the nursery programs vary. In general, however, the babies stay with their mothers for one to three years. The mothers, previously screened for drugs, mental health and behavioral problems, must be free of abusive charges, willing to participate in pre-natal and post-partum care, and must be eligible for release by the time the baby has to leave the institution. Space limitations in the nurseries result in many more women being denied, than awarded, this opportunity.

Each of these 11 nursery programs claims a high success rate (low recidivism) for the mothers as compared with the particular state's recidivism (return to prison) rate.

E. TOXIC SHAME AND HUMILIATION.

Definition: Toxic Shame is the feeling of being flawed and diminished and never measuring up. Toxic shame feels much worse than guilt. With guilt, you've done something wrong, but you can repair that...with toxic shame, (you feel like) there's something wrong with you and there's nothing you can do about it; you are inadequate and defective.

(John Bradshaw. *Healing the Shame that Binds You*. Deerfield Beach FL: Health Communications, Inc. 2005).

In this book, you have read life stories which illustrate the shame and humiliation (now known as adverse childhood experiences [ACE's]) endured by women prisoners during their childhood/teen years. It is that shame that propelled them into behaviors (running away from home, prostitution, self-medicating on illegal drugs, stealing, etc.) intended to self-rescue but which our society condemns as violations of laws.

Examining the "why's" of these self-rescue behaviors would place society and the CJS on the path of helping incarcerated women overcome their traumas, grow in self-esteem, and actualize their giftedness.

But we seem, unwittingly, to disregard the "why's". We place the proverbial cart before the horse, jailing the women instead of helping them.

Once they're in jail, the humiliations continue. Women reported to me that some facilities provided insufficient toilet paper and menstrual products. On occasion they were "locked down" if a CO saw menstrual refuse on their uniforms before they had time to change clothes. One of my student's menstrual period began during class. Before she knew it, blood had seeped through her underclothes onto her uniform. Once she was out of the classroom, she had to back out past the floor guards until she reached the door of Pod C where she was housed.

Humiliations suffered by trans-gender women are even worse than those endured by cisgender women and women with a lesbian orientation. Although PREA mandates that transgender prisoners be assigned to male or female housing on a case-by-case basis, giving "serious consideration" to the prisoner's sense of where she would be safer, state operated carceral facilities often ignore the law.

For example, St. Louis County police arrested Camilla, a trans-woman on a separate offense after she had been released from prison. She told me that, although she had asked to be placed with women in the prison, officers kept her in solitary confinement for two full years. "The loneliness almost killed me" she said.

TWENTY-FOUR:
A CRY FOR MERCY

*I*n the introduction to this book, I wrote "statistics are like flashlights. They illuminate one corner of a situation, leaving the rest in darkness." So it is with our Criminal Justice System (CJS).

The CJS focuses attention on the WHO's and WHAT's of criminal behavior, failing to unmask the WHY's. Lack of focus on the WHY's blinds us to the foundational problems that incubate women's crimes: the traumas that wound young girls and teens, drawing them into unhealthy relationships, drugs, prostitution, crime and jail.

I hope that the stories of these traumatized children, now justice-involved-women:

- opened your eyes to their tormented childhoods,
- shocked you with the horrors of carceral life, and
- convinced you they need merciful healing, not punishment.

When I first began teaching incarcerated women in the early 1990's, my students were the first women in their families to be jailed. When I retired from this ministry in 2019, more than half of the women were second and third generation arrestees. Clearly, incarceration does not effectively eliminate crime.

Alcoholics Anonymous has a saying: "Insanity is doing the same thing over and over while expecting a different result." It begs the question: Can we not see that punishment is an ineffective, mindless approach to crime prevention? Why, then, do we allow, and even advocate for, punishment in response to crime? Is our CJS – are our legislators – unaware of healthy alternatives?

Following arrest and the processes involved in freeing a woman's body from drugs, healing work should begin.

What if, instead of "stoning" women's "whoreness," we, "societal advocates," guided them toward wholeness? What if, instead of jailing them for breaking laws, we helped them break addictive habits? What if, instead of sending them to costly (state average of $34,274/year) carceral facilities, we educated them and trained them for jobs?

Yes, and what if we transformed our jails and prisons into wholistic centers where these women could become physically healthy, emotionally stable, financially self-supporting, and spiritually alive?

In today's USA, incarceration causes more problems than it solves. The stories and information in this book testify to that fact. In addition, statistics show that corrections officers – men and women employed by these facilities – commit suicide at higher rates than people in other occupations. Can we deny that prison jobs are unhealthy?

Voices are currently debating the future of prisons. Should they be abolished or reformed. I stand on the side of abolition, with the understanding that the few women who commit grievous offenses must be separated from the public and housed where they can heal their lives, repair the harms their addictive behavior inflicts on others, and move toward healthy living. There's a name for it: transformative justice.

Transformative justice would replace punitive processes. It works in other countries. Why not in the U.S.? (NOTE: The U.S. has a higher percentage of incarcerated citizens, and those citizens are serving longer sentences than any other country in our world.) As of November 13, 2018, the numbers of girls and women incarcerated in the United States numbered 225,730:

Federal Facilities	16,000
State Prisons	99,000
Local Jails	89,000
Juvenile Facilities	14,000 (10-18 year olds)
Tribal Facilities	700
Military Facilities	30
Immigration Facilities	7,000

(Aleks Kajstura. *Women's Mass Incarceration: The Whole Pie, 2017*, A Prison Policy Initiative).

Most are imprisoned for non-violent crimes.

The violent crimes committed by the remainder – "the dangerous few" – fall into categories of assault, robbery, sexual assault, manslaughter and murder. We can sub-divide these violent crimes into five categories based on motivation.

1. hate crimes (against people identified as "other" – black, Jew, Moslem, and others),

2. crimes of greed and power (Mafia, terrorists, internet thieves, traffickers, gang leaders, and rapes committed by the "powerful and the elite,")

3. crimes of passion (domestic violence, victim retaliation, taking blame for boyfriend's crimes,

4. crimes of self-defense, and

5. crimes of necessity (crimes related to poverty, drug use disorders, and the underground economy.)

Rarely do women commit crimes in the first two (violent) categories. Those in the latter three categories would be candidates for the transformative processes. Those processes would help the women climb Maslow's Hierarchy of Needs, enabling them not just to survive, but to thrive.

The Maslow Hierarchy of Needs are:

1. Physiological and Basic Needs such as food, clothing, and shelter,

2. Safety and Security,

3. Love and Belonging,

4. Self-Esteem,

5. Self-Actualization.

(A.H. Maslow, *"A Theory of Human Motivation,"* Psychological Review. 50: (4), 370-96, 1943).

My work showed me that most of the justice-involved-women, as children, fell out of society's safety net. Life seldom, or only partially and inconsistently, provided their physiological need for food, clothing and shelter, or their need for safety and security. As teens, they sought love and belonging in unhealthy relationships where they misidentified or misunderstood "love and belonging" as "sex and belonging to". Once that happened, self-esteem and self-actualization evaporated, like mist, beyond their grasp.

Women respond differently to harms than do men. What we do to men, they generally repeat in their male relationships. Trash them and they will trash others. But if we trash women, we teach them to trash themselves. However, if we love them, they learn to love themselves.

How, then should we respond to justice-involved-women.

Scripture gives us the answer:

> "The Spirit of the Lord is upon (us) … has anointed (us) to proclaim good news to the poor… to proclaim freedom for the prisoners … and to set the oppressed free." (Lk 4:18, New International Version).

Greater life for the oppressed, boomerangs into greater life for everyone.

A few years ago, Pope Francis wrote:

> "We need a people capable of rediscovering
> the maternal womb of mercy.
> Without mercy we have little chance nowadays

of becoming a part of a world of

wounded persons (healed by) understanding and love."

(Pope Francis, Address in Brazil on 27 July, 2013. Quoted in Newsmax,

Sept. 05, 2021).

Pope Francis's words ring true to life. Unless mercy penetrates our individual and societal justice, we have little hope of growing into a transformed people capable of making this world a better place.

CHAPTER 25:
AN AFTER-WORD

*A*lternatives to incarceration are available in a limited number of U.S. cities. The Center for Women in Transition (CWIT) in St. Louis, which began with a foundational grant from the Sisters of Mercy (now Sisters of Mercy of the Americas), currently works with 150 justice-involved-women per year. Since its founding in 1997, it has served over 2,300 women. CWIT's mission states: "The Center for Women in Transition, founded on restorative justice, offers comprehensive wrap-around services, including supportive housing; case management; life skills education; behavioral health services; peer support services; provision of basic necessities including food, transportation, and clothing; vocational services; and mentor partnerships."

If you feel called to support this ministry, your contributions will be gratefully received. Please send checks to CWIT, 7716 South Broadway, St. Louis MO 63111. TEL (314) 771-5207. cwit@cwitstl.org